Study Guide

to accompany

Foundations of Microbiology

Third Edition

Kathleen Park Talaro
Pasadena City College

Arthur Talaro

Prepared by
Jackie Butler
Grayson County College

Contributing Author
Katherine Whelchel
Anoka-Ramsey Community College

 **WCB McGraw-Hill**

Boston   Burr Ridge, IL   Dubuque, IA   Madison, WI   New York   San Francisco   St. Louis
Bangkok   Bogotá   Caracas   Lisbon   London   Madrid
Mexico City   Milan   New Delhi   Seoul   Singapore   Sydney   Taipei   Toronto

WCB/McGraw-Hill

A Division of The McGraw-Hill Companies

Study Guide to accompany
FOUNDATIONS IN MICROBIOLOGY, THIRD EDITION

Copyright ©1999 by The McGraw-Hill Companies, Inc. All rights reserved.
Previous edition(s) copyright year 1996 by Wm. C. Brown Publishers.
Printed in the United States of America.

The contents of, or parts thereof, may be reproduced for use with
FOUNDATIONS IN MICROBIOLOGY by Kathleen Park Talaro and Arthur Talaro,
provided such reproductions bear copyright notice and may not be reproduced in any
form for any other purpose without permission of the publisher.

2 3 4 5 6 7 8 9 0 BKM/BKM 9 0 9

ISBN 0-697-35455-5

www.mhhe.com

Contents

INTRODUCTION

You are beginning an introductory microbiology course. You have purchased your text and have bought, or are thinking of buying, this study guide. You are probably interested in the benefits of a study guide for this course. This study guide has been designed to assist you in several ways. Complete the exercises and you should be able to:

1. increase your recall of key terms and concepts in microbiology;
2. increase your understanding of the relationship among key concepts in microbiology;
3. improve your ability to reason with microbiological concepts to solve both familiar and novel problems;
4. increase your knowledge of significant microorganisms and their medical importance;
5. improve your ability to monitor and assess your own study skills and understanding of microbiology.

In this study guide you will find the text chapters divided into sections, with a key concept for focus on each particular section. You will find learning objectives. Keyed to these objectives are various exercises to provide you with practice answering typical test questions and to assist you in diagnosing your strengths and weaknesses as you study. Before jumping into chapter 1 you might want to finish reading this introduction, which includes who I am, who I think you are, and further suggestions for studying microbiology.

I have spent many hours pondering the kinds of problems you might have in studying microbiology. Since I will be your study partner for the next several weeks, we may as well get acquainted.

I have taught microbiology and anatomy and physiology for health care professionals at the two-year college level for many years. Besides lecturing, I have designed and taught laboratory classes in these subject areas. My professional training is in microbiology and education. My years of teaching experience have supplied me with firsthand knowledge of the specific problems and challenges you will encounter in this course.

If you are like many of my current and former students, this is your first microbiology course and possibly your first college science course. Your reasons for taking this course vary, but you are most likely enrolled because it is required. I have written this study guide with you in mind. Hopefully, you will find it "user friendly."

This study guide has been designed to help you obtain the most information from your textbook, whether your instructor follows the topics in the textbook or prefers to lecture on topics not covered in the textbook, using the text as a back-up reference.

Besides using the study guide regularly, you should attend the course lectures and labs regularly. Read ahead and study each day. Be systematic and organized. I have found that many students benefit from studying together. The chance to talk about and practice using the new vocabulary and ideas incorporates this subject into your everyday life. Look around your classroom, and initiate a study group. (It's a great way to make friends!) After working through a chapter in the study guide, get together with your group and review the areas where you have weaknesses and misunderstandings. You may know a lot more than you thought!

The introduction would not be complete without certain acknowledgments. I want to acknowledge the patience and understanding of my husband, Dale, and children, Rosanna and Cade. They have proofed, typed, and encouraged every step of the way. I also want to acknowledge my students—past, present, and future—for their critiques, enthusiasm, and stimulus to keep on writing.

1 The Main Themes of Microbiology

OVERVIEW

Microbiology, the study of organisms generally not visible to the human eye, is a relatively "young" science with most of the discoveries having taken place in the last 300 years. Bacteria, fungi, viruses, protozoa, algae, and helminths, all of which may be harmful or beneficial, are included in the study of microbiology. An organized system for classifying and naming microorganisms is helpful towards identifying each particular microorganism.

I. INTRODUCTION

Concept: Humans are greatly affected by microbes that act both adversely and beneficially.

> **Objective 1.** Describe the harmful effects of microbes.
> **Objective 2.** Identify beneficial activities of microbes.

A. Define pathogen.

B. List and describe major beneficial activities of microbes.

II. THE SCOPE OF MICROBIOLOGY

Concept: Usually magnification is necessary to view the organisms included in this specialized area of biology.

> **Objective 1.** Discuss microbiology and the microbes it encompasses.
> **Objective 2.** Explain the practical applications of microbiology.

A. Define microbiology.

List the major biological groups of organisms studied by microbiologists.

Which characteristics of microorganisms make them more accessible and ideal subjects for study?

B. List and describe the practical uses of microbiology.

III. THE CHARACTERISTICS OF MICROORGANISMS

Concept: Microorganisms may be cellular (procaryotic or eucaryotic) or noncellular (viruses).

   Objective 1.   Describe the general characteristics of microbes.

A. What is the primary difference between a procaryotic cell and a eucaryotic cell?

   Is a virus a cell? Explain your answer.

   What is the size range of microorganisms?

   Contrast free-living organisms and parasites.

IV. THE HISTORICAL FOUNDATIONS OF MICROBIOLOGY

Concept: The past 300 years of microbiology encompass the development of the microscope, the rise of the scientific method, the germ theory of disease, and the origins of modern microbiological techniques.

   Objective 1.   Discuss the importance of the microscope for studying microbiology.
   Objective 2.   Explain the scientific method.
   Objective 3.   Identify famous scientists and relate them to their discoveries.

A. Explain how the invention of the microscope influenced the science of microbiology.

B. Describe the scientific method as a process. Identify the key steps in the scientific method.

   What is a control group?

   What purpose does the control group serve?

C. Matching.

_____ He established a series of proofs that determined if an
     organism caused disease and which disease it caused.
_____ He invented pasteurization.
_____ He discovered heat-resistant bacterial endospores.
_____ He introduced aseptic technique.
_____ His first microscope could magnify the image up to
     300 times.
_____ He observed that mothers whose babies were delivered
     by physicians coming directly from the autopsy room
     developed more infections.
_____ He observed that mothers who gave birth at home
     experienced fewer infections.

a. Leeuwenhoek
b. Cohn
c. Holmes
d. Semmelweiss
e. Lister
f. Pasteur
g. Koch

V. TAXONOMY: ORGANIZING, CLASSIFYING, AND NAMING MICROORGANISMS

Concept: Carl von Linné devised a system of taxonomy for organizing, classifying, and naming living
things to prevent chaos in scientific studies and to allow workers in many biological fields to
know they were discussing the same organism.

Objective 1. Identify the levels of taxonomy.
Objective 2. Discuss binomial nomenclature.
Objective 3. Explain the rationale for dividing living organisms into kingdoms for further
classification.

A. List in order the levels of classification beginning with the most general.

(*K*ing *P*hillip *C*ame *O*ver *F*rom *G*reat *S*pain.)

B. Identify an advantage of using standardized nomenclature over common names.

Write the scientific name staphylococcus (genus) aureus (species) correctly.

List the inspirations for the varied scientific names of microbes.

C. Characterize the member organisms and provide an example organism of the five basic kingdoms as
proposed by Robert Whittaker:

Procaryotae (Monera)—

Protista—

Myceteae (Fungi)—

Animalia—

Plantae—

Where do viruses fit into the kingdom classification?

VI. SELF-TEST

1. All microbes are harmful, in that they are all pathogenic and cause disease.
   a. True
   b. False

2. Attributes that make microbes ideal subjects for study include all *except*
   a. their relative simplicity.
   b. their rapid rate of reproduction.
   c. their complexity.
   d. their adaptability.
   e. none of the above.

3. All eucaryotes are microorganisms.
   a. True
   b. False

4. Most microbes are measured in
   a. meters.
   b. decimeters.
   c. centimeters.
   d. micrometers.
   e. kilometers.

5. The early observations that meat left out in the open would soon "produce" maggots was used to support the idea of
   a. spontaneous generation.
   b. biogenesis.
   c. abiogenesis.
   d. a and b above.
   e. a and c above.

6. Experimental variables that can hypothetically affect or change an outcome include
   a. physical factors.
   b. chemical factors.
   c. biological factors.
   d. all of the above.
   e. none of the above.

7. An important guideline in the acceptance of a hypothesis is that the experimental data must be published and repeated by other investigators in that field.
   a. True
   b. False

8. In the taxonomic hierarchy, the category beneath order and above genus is
   a. kingdom.
   b. phylum.
   c. class.
   d. family.
   e. species.

9. In the name *Escherichia coli, Escherichia* is the
   a. species.
   b. genus.
   c. family.
   d. order.
   e. class.

10. Viruses are classified as belonging to the kingdom
    a. Procaryote.
    b. Protista.
    c. Myceteae.
    d. Animalia.
    e. none of the above.

11. The following are all cellular microbes except
    a. fungi.
    b. protozoa.
    c. algae.
    d. bacteria.
    e. viruses.

12. Which of the following is a scientific name?
    a. Legionnaire's bacterium
    b. *Legionella pneumophilia*
    c. Coliform
    d. Coccus
    e. Spirilla

13. Which of the following is not a kingdom in the five-kingdom system?
    a. Virus
    b. Procaryotae
    c. Myceteae
    d. Plantae
    e. Protista

14. A clear association between contamination from the autopsy room and infection in the maternity room was demonstrated by
    a. Cohn.
    b. Semmelweis.
    c. Lister.
    d. Pasteur.
    e. Wasserman.

15. Proof that microbes cause disease was provided by
    a. Cohn.
    b. Semmelweis.
    c. Lister.
    d. Pasteur.
    e. Wasserman.

16. Which of the following is a beneficial activity of microorganisms?
    a. some microorganisms participate in food production
    b. some microorganisms produce medicine (antibiotics)
    c. some microorganisms are used in sewage treatment
    d. some microorganisms produce human hormones
    e. all of the above

17. The scientific name *Clostridium tetani* is written correctly.
    a. True
    b. False

18. The microscope was invented by Theodor Schwann.
    a. True
    b. False

19. Which of the following is not part of the study of microbiology?
    a. bacteria
    b. fungi
    c. viruses
    d. insects
    e. helminths

20. Taxonomic hierarchy from the largest, most general, to the smaller, more specific, includes
    a. species, genus, family, order, class, phylum, kingdom.
    b. species, family, genus, class, order, phylum, kingdom.
    c. kingdom, phylum, class, order, family, genus, species
    d. kingdom, phylum, order, class, genus, family, species.
    e. none of the above.

2 From Atoms to Cells: A Chemical Connection

OVERVIEW

A basic understanding of chemistry is important for the study of living things. Composed of chemicals, living things are affected and controlled by the chemical interactions within their cells.

I. INTRODUCTION

Concept: Ultimately, all biological events involve chemistry.

II. ATOMS, BONDS, AND MOLECULES: FUNDAMENTAL BUILDING BLOCKS

Concept: Matter occupies space, has mass, and is composed of protons (+), neutrons (neutral), and electrons (–) arranged within atoms.

> **Objective 1.** Discuss the significance of the atomic weight, the atomic number, and the electron orbitals of an element.
> **Objective 2.** Compare the various atomic bonds formed in the production of a compound.
> **Objective 3.** Correlate chemical reactions with their appropriate equations.
> **Objective 4.** Explain what is meant by the terms solute and solvent with respect to various solutions.
> **Objective 5.** Summarize the principles of pH.
> **Objective 6.** Contrast organic and inorganic compounds.

A. Define atomic weight.

Since elements, as they occur in nature, do not carry an overall charge and the atomic number of the element is based upon the number of protons, the element would have an equal number of _____.

How do isotopes differ from the naturally occurring elements?

Electrons orbit the nucleus (protons and neutrons) of the atom in an energy sphere called a shell. The shells fill from the inside (those closest to the nucleus) out. The maximum number of electrons that fill the
first shell =
second shell =
third shell =
fourth shell =
The number of electrons in the outermost orbital is the valence and determines reactivity among atoms forming different types of bonds.

B. Describe the formation and give an example of a(an):

covalent bond—

ionic bond—

hydrogen bond—

Define:

anion—

cation—

electrolyte—

C. Write a generalized equation, indicating reactants and products, for the following types of reactions:

synthesis—

decomposition—

exchange—

reversible—

D. Define:

solution—

solute—

solvent—

Explain the correlation between solute and solvent when discussing the concentration of a solution.

E. Matching.

____ compound releases hydroxyl ions   a.   acid
____ compound releases hydrogen ions   b.   base
____ pH of 0 to 6.99   c.   neutral
____ pH of 7.00
____ pH of 7.01 to 14
____ compound with coexisting acid and base
____ salt

F. Characterize (include examples of):

inorganic compounds—

organic compounds—

III. MACROMOLECULES: SUPERSTRUCTURES OF LIFE

Concept: Organic compounds comprising living things can be divided into four groups of polymers: carbohydrates, lipids, proteins, and nucleic acids.

Objective 1. Characterize and discuss the functions of carbohydrates.
Objective 2. Characterize and discuss the functions of lipids.
Objective 3. Characterize and discuss the functions of proteins.
Objective 4. Characterize and discuss the functions of nucleic acids.

A. Distinguish between:

monosaccharides—

disaccharides—

polysaccharides—

List the various functions of carbohydrates.

B. Distinguish between:

triglycerides—

phospholipids—

steroids—

waxes—

List the various functions of lipids.

C. Distinguish between:

amino acid—

dipeptide—

polypeptide—

protein—

Describe protein structure:

primary structure—

secondary structure—

tertiary structure—

quaternary structure—

List the various functions of proteins.

D.   Distinguish between:

deoxyribonucleic acid (DNA)—

ribonucleic acid (RNA)—

adenosine triphosphate (ATP)—

List the components of a nucleotide.

List the various functions of nucleic acids.

IV. CELLS: WHERE CHEMICALS COME TO LIFE

Concept: The cell, the fundamental unit of life, is a huge aggregate of atoms producing the characteristics of life.

   Objective 1.   Differentiate between procaryotic and eucaryotic cells.
   Objective 2.   Enumerate and describe the biological activities or properties of living entities.

A.   List the common characteristics of cells.

Contrast procaryotic and eucaryotic cells.

B. Briefly discuss these biological activities of living cells:

reproduction—

metabolism—

motility or irritability—

protection and storage—

transport—

V. SELF-TEST

1. The atomic number of chlorine (Cl) is 17 and the atomic weight is 35.5. How many electrons are present in the third shell of the atom?
   a. 2
   b. 7
   c. 8
   d. 17
   e. 18

2. A combination of two or more different elements in a certain ratio is
   a. an atom.
   b. a molecule.
   c. a compound.
   d. a macromolecule.
   e. none of the above.

3. When the atoms shared by elements bonding covalently are not equally shared (asymmetrical distribution), the molecule is termed
   a. polar.
   b. nonpolar.

4. $C_6H_{12}O_6$ is the structural formula for glucose.
   a. True
   b. False

5. Reactants are
   a. atoms.
   b. elements.
   c. chemicals.
   d. molecules entering or starting a reaction.
   e. substances left by a reaction.

6. Functional groups are accessory molecules that bind to
   a. acids.
   b. bases.
   c. salts.
   d. inorganic compounds.
   e. organic compounds.

7. Saturated fats
   a. have all carbons single bonded and are of liquid consistency.
   b. have at least one C–C double bond and are solid.
   c. have at least one C–C double bond and are of liquid consistency.
   d. have all carbons single bonded and are solid.
   e. are none of the above.

8. Denaturing a protein by heat, acid, and alcohol changes the
   a. primary structure.
   b. secondary structure.
   c. tertiary structure.
   d. quaternary structure.
   e. all of the above.

9. Which of the following is mismatched (compound—subunit)?
   a. carbohydrate—monosaccharides
   b. triglyceride—fatty acids and glycerol
   c. protein—amino acids
   d. nucleic acid—nucleotides
   e. none of the above.

10. Replication is the process of
    a. duplicating DNA.
    b. duplicating RNA.
    c. duplicating ATP.
    d. duplicating cells.
    e. none of the above.

11. As the pH goes toward 0, the
    a. number of hydrogen ions increases.
    b. solution becomes more acidic.
    c. solution becomes more basic.
    d. both a and b.
    e. both a and c.

12. The two strands of DNA are held together by
    a. disulfide linkages.
    b. hydrogen bonding.
    c. carbon bonds.
    d. electrostatic forces.
    e. N linkages.

13. An acid and a base will react to form a salt and
    a. a gas.
    b. an ion.
    c. water.
    d. a metal.
    e. an acid.

14. The number of neutrons in an atom of fluorine, atomic number = 9 and atomic weight = 19, is
    a. 8.
    b. 9.
    c. 10.
    d. 7.
    e. 2.

15. Proteins consist of chains of
    a. monosaccharides.
    b. fatty acids.
    c. glycerol.
    d. amino acids.
    e. nucleotides.

16. Carbohydrates are made up of monosaccharides each containing carbon, hydrogen, oxygen, and phosphorus.
    a. True
    b. False

17. Lipid bonds between fatty acids are called peptide bonds.
    a. True
    b. False

18. All procaryotic and eucaryotic cells have the same organelles.
    a. True
    b. False

19. Compounds that always contain carbon are
    a. organic.
    b. inorganic.
    c. ionic.
    d. unstable.
    e. none of the above.

20. A pH of 7 means that a solution is
    a. acidic.
    b. basic.
    c. neutral.

3 Tools of the Laboratory: The Methods for Studying Microorganisms

OVERVIEW

Though studying microscopic organisms is fraught with unique problems, microbiologists have developed and refined technology to detect and identify microorganisms of all types. Inoculation of any one of a number of types of media, followed by incubation will give isolated (pure cultures) organisms. These organisms are then prepared for inspection with a light microscope or some modified form of the light microscope. Biochemical and genetic tests further aid in the identification of the microorganisms.

I.   INTRODUCTION

Concept: Special media for isolating the microbe, microscopes for observing it, and numerous biochemical and genetic tests are used to detect pathogens. Public health authorities are especially concerned with those pathogens affecting the fitness and safety of food.

II.   METHODS FOR CULTURING MICROORGANISMS

Concept: Microbiologists use the techniques of inoculation, incubation, isolation, inspection, and identification to separate invisible microbes from mixed populations and grow them under artificial conditions for study.

Objective 1.   Describe the unique problems microbiologists confront when studying microorganisms.

Objective 2.   Distinguish between pure, mixed, and contaminated cultures.

Objective 3.   Describe two isolation procedures to achieve a pure culture.

Objective 4.   Discuss the various physical states of media.

Objective 5.   Discuss the chemical content of various media.

Objective 6.   Describe different media with respect to function.

Objective 7.   Identify and describe techniques used in the cultivation of microbes.

A.   List the problems of studying such small subjects (microorganisms).

B.   Discuss similarities and differences between pure, mixed, and contaminated cultures.

C.   Explain the basis for the reasoning that an individual colony of bacteria is a pure culture of that particular type of microbe.

Contrast streak plate vs. pour plate techniques for isolating microorganisms.

D. List and describe the physical states of media.

Name a solidifying agent commonly used in media preparation.

E. Characterize the following:

synthetic media—

nonsynthetic media—

F. Complete the chart.

Media	Description	Function
general purpose		
enriched		
selective		
differential		
reducing		
carbohydrate fermentation		
transport		
assay		
enumeration		

G. Matching. (Answers may be used more than once.)

___ makes a culture (observable growth) of microbes by using a sterile tool to introduce the organism into a sterile medium

___ separates different types of microorganisms

___ macroscopic—examines colony (large mass of microorganisms), size, shape, color, texture

___ culture is placed at a temperature to facilitate microbial growth, usually 20°–40°C

___ microscopic—examines individual cell morphology

___ microbes multiply to produce visible growth

___ biochemical analyses to determine nutrient requirements, temperature and gas requirements, and mechanisms for deriving energy

a. inoculation
b. incubation
c. isolation
d. inspection
e. identification

List two effective methods for destroying microorganisms for disposal.

III. THE MICROSCOPE: WINDOW ON AN INVISIBLE REALM

Concept: The microscope is an essential tool for the study of microorganisms; therefore, it is important to understand some essentials of microscopy and specimen preparation.

Objective 1.   Explain the use of refraction to produce an enlarged image.
Objective 2.   Illustrate the importance of adequate magnification, resolution, and clarity of image to the effectiveness of the microscope.
Objective 3.   Discuss the variations on the optical microscope.
Objective 4.   Describe the various methods employed in specimen preparation for viewing with the optical microscope.

A.   How is an image formed when an object is illuminated with light and viewed through a spherical lens?

What determines the degree to which an image viewed through a convex lens is enlarged?

B.   What is the total magnification of a specimen viewed through a 10x ocular lens and a 45x objective lens?

Define resolution.

What is the purpose of the oil applied to the slide when viewing the specimen under the oil immersion objective?

List four factors influencing the clarity of image.

C. Fill in the puzzle.

Across
2. Microscope contrasts specimen against a gray background. It is used for observing the internal cellular detail of live specimens.
4. Microscope produces a white field and a dark specimen. It is used for observing live, preserved, and stained specimens.
6. Microscope uses an electron beam to form an image of the specimen.
8. Microscope uses ultraviolet rays as the illumination source.

Down
1. Microscope produces a dark field and a bright specimen. It is used for observing live, unstained specimens.
3. Abbreviation for an electron microscope that scans and magnifies the external surface of the specimen to produce a three-dimensional image.
5. Microscope produces brightly colored, highly contrasting, three-dimensional images of live specimens.
7. Abbreviation for an electron microscope used to view preserved material in finest detail under very high magnification.

D. List and detail the processes for preparing live specimens for viewing with the microscope.

Explain the purpose(s) for fixation of a smear.

Contrast negative and positive staining.

Contrast simple and differential staining.

Discuss the following differential and special staining techniques:

Differential:

gram staining—

acid-fast staining—

endospore staining—

Special:

capsule staining—

flagellar staining—

IV. SELF-TEST

1. A contaminated culture
   a. grows only a single known species.
   b. holds two or more known species.
   c. has unwanted microbes of unknown species.
   d. is all of the above.
   e. is none of the above.

2. A colony is a discrete mound of cells of two or more different species.
   a. True
   b. False

3. Agar, a complex polysaccharide used as a media solidifying agent, is a nutrient digested (metabolized) by most bacteria.
   a. True
   b. False

4. A medium that contains bile salts, lactose, and neutral red is
   a. a general purpose.
   b. enriched.
   c. selective.
   d. differential.
   e. selective and differential.

5. Incubators may control the temperature and _____, important conditions necessary for the growth of microbes in culture.
   a. pH
   b. nutrients
   c. atmospheric gas content
   d. all of the above
   e. none of the above

6. The factor that most limits the clarity of a microscope's image is its
   a. cost.
   b. magnification.
   c. objective lens.
   d. resolving power.
   e. size.

7. A compound microscope has a system of _____ magnifying len(s).
   a. one
   b. two
   c. three
   d. four
   e. none of the above

8. This type of microscope is used to view live, unstained *T. pallidum* in a mucus specimen.
   a. bright field
   b. dark field
   c. fluorescence
   d. transmission electron
   e. scanning electron

9. Basic dyes have what type of charge?
   a. positive
   b. negative
   c. neutral

10. The _____ stain guides the selection of the correct drug for an infection.
    a. flagellar
    b. capsule
    c. endospore
    d. acid-fast
    e. gram

11. Five basic techniques to manipulate, grow, examine, and characterize microorganisms include all *except*:
    a. inoculation.
    b. incubation.
    c. isolation.
    d. inhalation.
    e. inspection.

12. Culture media are contained in test tubes, flasks, or
    a. beakers.
    b. crucibles.
    c. pipettes.
    d. Petri plates.
    e. all of the above.

13. An axenic culture is a(an)
    a. pure culture.
    b. mixed culture.
    c. contaminated culture.
    d. identified culture.
    e. none of the above.

14. One difference between the streak plate method and the pour plate method is that in the pour plate technique some of the colonies will develop in the medium itself and not just on the surface.
    a. True
    b. False

15. Nonliquefiable solid media include
    a. rice grains.
    b. cooked meat.
    c. potato slices.
    d. eggs.
    e. all of the above.

16. Complex media (nonsynthetic) is chemically definable.
    a. True
    b. False

17. Bacteria that require growth factors and complex nutrients are called
    a. aerobes.
    b. anaerobes.
    c. pathogens.
    d. fastidious.
    e. complex.

18. The largest microbiological culture collection can be found at the
    a. Centers for Disease Control in Atlanta, Georgia.
    b. American Type Culture Collection in Rockville, Maryland.
    c. your local hospital.
    d. your college's microbiology lab.
    e. all of the above.

19. Shorter wavelengths provide better resolution, so some microscopes use this color of filter to limit the longer wavelengths from entering the specimen.
    a. yellow
    b. red
    c. blue
    d. green
    e. purple

20. Variations of the light (visible light) microscope include all except the
    a. bright-field microscope.
    b. dark-field microscope.
    c. phase contrast microscope.
    d. interference microscope.
    e. fluorescence microscope.

4 Procaryotic Profiles: The Bacteria and Archaea

OVERVIEW

Procaryotic cells are simple in structure. They demonstrate considerable variation in shapes, arrangements, and sizes. Preferably studied in pure culture, a variety of techniques—both microscopic and macroscopic—are used to identify and classify these unicellular organisms.

I. INTRODUCTION

Concept: Abundant and ubiquitous, procaryotic cells are essential to our existence. Knowledge of structure and behavior of procaryotic cells aids in understanding the interactions between us and the procaryotic cells.

II. THE STRUCTURE OF A GENERALIZED PROCARYOTIC CELL

Concept: The procaryotic cell, the least complex of all cells, can be broken down into a variety of structures, each of which serves a specific function.

Objective 1. List and describe the parts of the procaryotic cell.
Objective 2. State the function of each procaryotic cell structure.
Objective 3. Distinguish between those parts that are universal to all procaryotes and those that are not always present.
Objective 4. Describe the structure of the rigid procaryotic cell wall and distinguish between gram-positive and gram-negative cell walls.
Objective 5. Distinguish between bacterial chromosomes and bacterial plasmids.
Objective 6. Describe the conditions that cause endospore formation, then demonstrate an understanding of the processes of sporulation and germination.

A. Complete the chart on the following page.

B. Fill in the blanks.

1. The procaryotic cell wall is relatively rigid due to a giant polymeric molecule, _____, composed of a repeating framework of long glycan chains cross-linked by short peptide fragments.

2. Classify the following as components of gram-positive or gram-negative cell walls:

   a. techoic acid and lipotechoic acid _____

   b. lipopolysaccharide _____

   c. numerous sheets of peptidoglycan _____

d. thin shell of peptidoglycan _____

e. chemical sieve, protein channels _____

Describe the cell wall structure of mycoplasmas, archaea and L forms. Why can't these microorganisms be classified as gram-positive or gram-negative bacteria?

Structure	Description	Function	A/S*
Appendages: 1. flagellum (pl. flagella)			S
2.	modified flagella, entire structure enclosed between cell wall and cell membrane		
3.		tend to stick to each other and to surfaces, clinging	
4. pilus (pl. pili)			
Cell envelope: 5.	coating of macromolecules (slime layer, capsule)		
6.		accounts for the shape of the cell, protective, structural support	
7. cell membrane			A
Internal contents: 8.	gelatinous solution composed of water and nutrients		
9.		hereditary material of bacteria	
10. ribosomes			
11.	composed of energy-rich organic substances		
12.		facilitate bacterial survival under hostile conditions	

*A = always present
S = sometimes present

C. How are bacterial plasmids different from bacterial chromosomes?

D. What conditions preclude bacterial endospore formation?

Grandmother has picked green beans from her garden. In the process of washing the green beans before canning, she leaves a small amount of soil on the beans. (The soil contains an endospore-forming organism—*Clostridium botulinum*.) She places the beans in a Mason jar, and puts the jar in her pressure cooker to heat the contents prior to sealing. A few minutes later, she remembers an appointment and must leave the house immediately. She removes the jar of green beans from the pressure cooker, seals the jar, and places it at the back of a pantry shelf. She rushes off to her appointment. As the days go by, the bacteria multiply in the green beans in the jar on the shelf. They produce botulism neurotoxin.

When are the bacterial cells vegetative?

When did sporulation occur?

When did germination occur?

III. BACTERIAL SHAPES, ARRANGEMENTS, AND SIZES

Concept: The bacteria are unicellular organisms that come in a variety of shapes, arrangements, and sizes (visible with light microscopy).

Objective 1. Describe the various bacterial shapes.
Objective 2. Differentiate between the various bacterial cell arrangements or groupings.

A. Draw the bacterial shape:

coccus—

bacillus—

coccobacillus—

vibrio—

spirillum—

spirochete—

B. Identify the bacterial arrangements.

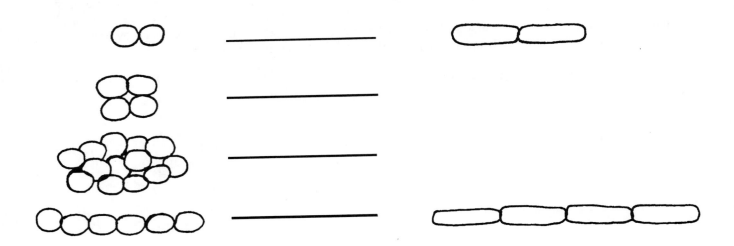

IV. BACTERIAL IDENTIFICATION AND CLASSIFICATION SYSTEMS

Concept: Once an organism is cultivated and isolated, a classification system is used in differentiating and identifying the unknown species.

Objective 1. List and discuss methods of bacterial identification to the level of genus and species.
Objective 2. Compare and contrast three proposed systems of bacterial classification (*Bergey's Manual of Systematic Bacteriology* and medically important bacteria).

A. Matching.

_____ microscopic morphology
_____ macroscopic morphology
_____ physiological characteristics
_____ serological analysis
_____ chemical analysis
_____ genetic analysis

a. testing bacterial cultures with known, specific antibody
b. size/shape of cells, gram stain reaction, special structures
c. testing DNA for G/C content
d. testing for types of specific chemical substances possessed by a bacterium
e. tests determining enzyme and nutritional characteristics
f. appearance of colonies on nutrient, selective, and differential media

B. Name the four divisions of the kingdom Procaryotae, key characteristics of each, and two well-known genera in each.

Name and describe the eleven groups of bacteria based on similarities in the base sequence of rRNA.

Since the medically important families and genera of bacteria are not subdivided into taxonomic ranks as per *Bergey's Manual,* what is the basis for subdividing?

V. SURVEY OF BACTERIAL GROUPS WITH UNUSUAL CHARACTERISTICS

Concept: Certain types of bacteria exhibit unusual qualities.

> **Objective 1.** Discuss unusual forms of medically significant bacteria as well as those not involved in human disease.

A. What characteristic would differentiate between the obligate parasites, rickettsias, and chlamydias?

Which type of bacterium naturally lacks a cell wall?

Match the organism to the disease it causes.

_____ atypical pneumonia
_____ trachoma
_____ STD (sexually transmitted disease)
_____ Rocky Mountain spotted fever

a. *Rickettsia*
b. *Chlamydia*
c. *Mycoplasma*

List some unusual bacteria not involved in human disease.

VI. SELF-TEST

1. Bacteria are ubiquitous; they are found
    a. in soil.
    b. associated with animals.
    c. in water.
    d. in all of the above locations.
    e. in none of the above locations.

2. All of the following are types of flagellar arrangement *except*
    a. amphitrichous.
    b. monotrichous.
    c. polytrichous.
    d. peritrichous.
    e. lophotrichous.

3. Cells take on different colors as a result of Gram staining because of
   a. differences in metabolism.
   b. differences in cell wall structure/composition.
   c. differences in shape.
   d. differences in habitat.
   e. all of the above.

4. Identify the organism by shape and arrangement of the cells.
   a. diplococcus
   b. diplobacillus
   c. streptococcus
   d. streptobacillus
   e. staphylococcus

5. Cell membrane functions include all *except*
   a. control nutrients' passage into the cell.
   b. control waste discharge.
   c. involvement in secretion.
   d. the site of metabolic activities.
   e. maintaining bacterial shape.

6. Which bacterial structure is involved in protein synthesis?
   a. ribosome
   b. granule
   c. inclusion
   d. endospore
   e. mesosome

7. Bacterial motility can be determined by
   a. direct visualization of stained flagella.
   b. placing a mass of cells in a semisolid agar medium.
   c. microscope with a hanging drop slide.
   d. all of the above.
   e. none of the above.

8. What is the function of a bacterial endospore?
   a. reproduction
   b. survival
   c. nutrition
   d. motility
   e. protein synthesis

9. Spirochetes differ from spirilla in all of the following ways *except*
   a. gram reaction.
   b. overall appearance.
   c. mode of locomotion.
   d. number of helical turns.
   e. spirilla are mostly harmless.

10. Besides staining, gram positives differ from gram negatives in
    a. their reaction to antibiotics.
    b. their reaction to disinfectants.
    c. their reaction to lysozyme.
    d. their interaction with human tissues.
    d. all of the above.

11. The rigidity of the procaryotic cell wall is due to the presence of
    a. cellulose.
    b. chitin.
    c. pectin.
    d. phospholipid.
    e. peptidoglycan.

12. A bacterium with surrounding flagella is called
    a. monotrichous.
    b. lophotrichous.
    c. peritrichous.
    d. amphitrichous.
    e. polytrichous.

13. Which of these is not found in all procaryotes?
    a. ribosomes
    b. DNA
    c. cell membrane
    d. cell wall
    e. cytoplasm

14. Which structure is used for conjugation (transfer of DNA)?
    a. fimbria
    b. pilus
    c. cell envelope
    d. capsule
    e. slime layer

15. The bacterial genus with no cell wall is
    a. *Staphylococcus*.
    b. *Bacillus*.
    c. *Clostridium*.
    d. *Mycoplasma*.
    e. *Escherichia*.

16. Which of the following is not a characteristic of the cell membrane?
    a. maintains cell shape
    b. composed of a phospholipid bilayer
    c. contains proteins
    d. selectively permeable
    e. all of the above

17. Which of the following statements about bacterial endospores is true?
    a. Endospores are for reproduction.
    b. Endospores allow a cell to survive environmental changes.
    c. Endospores are easily stained with the gram staining procedure.
    d. A cell produces one endospore and keeps growing.
    e. A cell produces many endospores at one time.

18. *Sporosarcina, Bacillus*, and _____ may form endospores.
    a. *Staphulococcus*
    b. *Streptococcus*
    c. *Clostridium*
    d. all spirilla
    e. all rods

19. Where is the axial filament of a spirochete located?
    a. outside the cell wall
    b. inside the cell membrane
    c. within the cytoplasm
    d. between the cell wall and cell membrane
    e. within the capsule

20. The function of the procaryotic glycocalyx is to
    a. provide cell shape.
    b. produce a gram reaction.
    c. act as a selectively permeable barrier.
    d. protect against water/nutrient loss and phagocytosis.
    e. none of the above.

5 Eucaryotic Cells and Microorganisms

OVERVIEW

Eucaryotic cells are more complex, possessing a membrane-bound nucleus as well as other organelles. Fungi, algae, protozoa, and helminths are all either unicellular of multicellular eucaryotes. Demonstrating great variation, these microorganisms are important in medicine, industry, and agriculture.

I. INTRODUCTION

Concept: Fungi, algae, protozoa, and helminths are all composed of the more complex eucaryotic cell.

II. FORM AND FUNCTION OF THE EUCARYOTIC CELL: EXTERNAL STRUCTURES AND INTERNAL STRUCTURES

Concept: The complex structure of the eucaryotic cell allows for versatile microorganisms with respect to available habitats and diverse styles of living (including unicellular, colonial, and multicellular).

Objective 1. List and describe the parts of the eucaryotic cell.
Objective 2. State the function of each eucaryotic cell structure.
Objective 3. Distinguish between those parts that are common to all eucaryotes and those that are not always present.

A. Complete the chart on the following page.

III. SURVEY OF EUCARYOTIC MICROORGANISMS

Concept: The Kingdom Myceteae is divided into the macroscopic fungi (mushrooms, puffballs, gill fungi) and the microscopic fungi (yeasts, molds).

Objective 1. Distinguish between the basic morphological types of fungal cells.
Objective 2. Describe the nutritional patterns of fungi.
Objective 3. Describe the colonial organization of the microscopic fungi.
Objective 4. List and summarize the reproductive spores of the microscopic fungi.
Objective 5. Discuss the classification of the microscopic fungi.
Objective 6. Describe fungal identification and cultivation.
Objective 7. Relate the significance of fungi to disease, as well as to their nonmedical economic impact.

Structure	Description	Function	A/S*
Appendages: 1. flagellum (pl. flagella)			
2.	shorter and more numerous		
Cell envelope: 3.		protection, adherence of cells to surfaces, receives signals	S
4. cell wall			
5.	bilayer of phospholipids in which proteins are embedded		
Organelles: 6.		contains the genetic information, regulates cell activities	
7. nucleolus			
8.	intricate passageway, may be embedded with ribosomes		
9.		packaging/transport	
10. lysosomes			
11.	membrane-bound sacs, contain liquid or solid		
12.		generate energy	
13. chloroplasts			S
14.	thin protein strands attached to cell membrane		
15.		maintain cell shape, spindle fibers—mitosis	
16. ribosomes			

*A = always present
S = sometimes present

A. Distinguish between:

yeast—

molds—

dimorphic—

B. (Organic or Inorganic) substrates are required by all fungi.

Saprobes feed upon:

Fungi are described as fastidious, i.e., highly selective in their choice of food.
True/False

C. Describe the appearance of a colony of yeast.

Describe the appearance of a colony of filamentous fungi.

Distinguish between a septate and nonseptate hypha.

What is the function of the vegetative hyphae (mycelia)?

What is the function of the aerial or fertile hyphae?

D. Match the following asexual (dominant phase) spores.

____ sporangiospores	a.	rectangular spore formed by septate hypha
____ conidia	b.	free spores not enclosed by a special spore-bearing sac
____ chlamydospore	c.	smaller/larger conidia, formed by same fungus under varying
____ arthrospore		conditions
____ phialospore	d.	formed by successive cleavages within a saclike head
____ porospore	e.	conidium grows out through small pores in sporogenous cell
____ blastospore	f.	spherical conidium formed by thickening of hyphal cell
____ micro/macroconidium	g.	spore produced by budding from a parent cell
	h.	conidium budded from mouth of vase-shaped sporogenous cell

Match the following sexual spores.

____ zygospores	a.	formed when two different strains or sexes conjugate
____ ascospores	b.	formed on the outside of a club-shaped cell, which results from the
____ basidiospores		fusion of mating types and formation of terminal cells
	c.	fusion of the two hypha tips of two opposite strains

With which type of spore (asexual/sexual) are the resulting organisms *not* genetically identical?

E. In the absence of an official classification scheme, medical mycology is acceptable for categorizing the Kingdom Myceteae. Complete the table below.

	Name	Sexual spores	Asexual spores	Habitat	Species
Phylum I					
Phylum II					
Phylum III					
Phylum IV					

F. Since fungi grow on almost any medium, why is it important to use a medium with a low pH when isolating a fungus?

G. Match the causative fungus to the common disease.

    ____ ringworm   a. *Histoplasma capsulatum*
    ____ athlete's foot   b. *Candida albicans*
    ____ yeast infection   c. *Trichophyton/Epidermophyton*
    ____ histoplasmosis

Contrast the positive and negative economic impacts of fungi.

Concept: The Kingdom Protista contains the microscopic algae and the protozoa.

    Objective 1. Characterize the algal cell by its habitat, reproduction, and significance to society.
    Objective 2. Characterize the protozoan cell by its nutritional pattern, habitat range, locomotion, and reproduction.
    Objective 3. Describe the general life cycle of most human parasites.
    Objective 4. Describe in detail the life cycle of select parasitic protozoans and helminths.
    Objective 5. Discuss the classification and identification of helminths.

A. Describe the typical algal cell.

Algae commonly inhabit _____ and _____ waters.

Algae reproduce asexually through _____, _____, and _____. Their sexual reproductive cycles are similar to _____.

List some algal contributions beneficial to society.

What is the primary medical threat from algae?

B. Distinguish between protozoan ectoplasm and endoplasm.

Discuss the various feeding habits of protozoans.

What is the main limiting factor for protozoan habitat?

Protozoans are motile by means of _____, _____,
or _____.

Define with respect to protozoans:

trophozoite—

cyst—

Fill in the chart.

	Form of motility	Form of reproduction	Examples
Mastigophora			
Sarcodina			
Ciliophora			
Sporozoa			

C. List the general stages in the life cycle of most human parasites.

Define vector.

D. Describe the life cycle of *Trypanosoma cruzi* (be sure to include the host(s), insect vector, and mode of transmission).

Describe the life cycle of *Entamoeba histolytica.*

Describe the life cycle of *Enterobius vermicularis.*

E. List the characteristics used to classify helminths.

Describe how helminths are identified in the laboratory.

1. *All* eucaryotic cells possess the following structures with the exception of
   a. a nucleus.
   b. mitochondria.
   c. chloroplasts.
   d. the Golgi apparatus.
   e. vacuoles.

2. The structure of eucaryotic flagella is much the same as the structure of procaryotic flagella.
   a. True
   b. False

3. The structure of the eucaryotic glycocalyx is much like that of the procaryotes'.
   a. True
   b. False

4. Fungal spores are responsible for
   a. multiplication.
   b. survival.
   c. variation.
   d. dissemination.
   e. all of the above.

5. Factors that influence human acquisition of protozoan infection include
   a. geographic area in which a person lives.
   b. stages in the life cycle of the parasite.
   c. both a and b.

6. All flatworms and roundworms are parasites.
   a. True
   b. False

7. The trematodes, or flukes, have flat, ovoid bodies.
   a. True
   b. False

8. The hermaphroditic worm has
   a. a well-developed digestive system.
   b. sex organs to produce sperm.
   c. sex organs to produce eggs.
   d. sex organs to produce both eggs and sperm.
   e. none of the above.

9. Their unique appearance allows identification of genus and often species by microscopic morphology alone.
   a. bacteria
   b. algae
   c. yeasts
   d. protozoans
   e. molds

10. Host–parasite relationships can be very broad, ranging from the "good" parasite (which causes little harm to the host) to the "bad" parasite (which causes severe damage and disease).
    a. True
    b. False

11. Which of the following is mismatched?
    a. endoplasmic reticulum—internal transport
    b. Golgi apparatus—secretion
    c. mitochondrion—energy production
    d. ribosome—food storage
    e. lysosome—digestive enzymes

12. The structure that is involved with RNA synthesis is the
    a. mitochondrion.
    b. nucleolus.
    c. Golgi apparatus.
    d. endoplasmic reticulum.
    e. vacuole.

13. Microtubules in the cytoskeleton of the eucaryotic cell are responsible for the streaming of the organelles and the formation of pseudopods by *Amoeba*.
    a. True
    b. False

14. Eucaryotic and procaryotic flagella are the same structures.
    a. True
    b. False

15. The kingdom Protista includes the algae and helminths.
    a. True
    b. False

16. Asexual fungal spores include all except
    a. sporangiospores.
    b. conidiospores.
    c. arthrospores.
    d. zygospores.
    e. blastospores.

17. Sabouraud's agar is used to isolate fungi from mixed samples because its low pH inhibits bacterial growth, but not most fungal growth.
    a. True
    b. False

18. True fungal pathogens
    a. attack persons who are already weakened in some way.
    b. infect animals only.
    c. infect even healthy persons.
    d. require a host to complete their life cycle.
    e. none of the above.

19. All protozoa are motile.
    a. True
    b. False

20. Protozoa are motile by
    a. pseudopods.
    b. flagella.
    c. cilia.
    d. all of the above.
    e. none of the above.

6 An Introduction to the Viruses

OVERVIEW

Viruses are noncellular, infectious particles that utilize the host cell's genetic machinery to produce new virus particles. For this reason they are called obligate intracellular parasites and must be cultured in living cells. Currently, treatment for viral disease is limited due to the difficulty in killing the virus while sparing the host cell. So vaccination and prevention are the best defenses against viral infection.

I. INTRODUCTION

Concept: Viruses are noncellular with intimate connections to their host cells.

II. THE SEARCH FOR THE ELUSIVE VIRUSES

Concept: The ultramicroscopic, infectious particles called viruses are exceptionally compact and simplistic in structure.

Objective 1. Explain why viruses are obligate intracellular parasites.
Objective 2. Compare the sizes of viruses to other organisms studied in this course.
Objective 3. Discuss and give examples of the various external coverings possessed by viral particles.
Objective 4. Describe and give examples of the various central core structures found within viral particles.

A. Describe how a virus uses a host cell to release quantities of new virus.

B. How small are viruses compared to procaryotes? eucaryotes?

C. External coverings of viral particles include both the _____, possessed by all viral particles and the _____, possessed by some viral particles.

Describe in detail the viral capsid.

Distinguish between helical and icosahedral viruses.

Name some examples of the following types of viruses:

naked (does not possess an envelope) helical viruses—

enveloped helical viruses—

naked icosahedral viruses—

enveloped icosahedral viruses—

Indicate the functions of the viral capsid/envelope.

Describe the more intricately structured, complex viruses (poxviruses and bacteriophages).

D. Viral particles contain only one type of nucleic acid, either DNA or RNA.
    True/False

Besides the nucleic acid core, viruses may contain _____ for specific operations within their host.

III. HOW VIRUSES ARE CLASSIFIED AND NAMED

Concept: Since viruses are not cells, the Kingdom system of nomenclature is not appropriate. For many years, viruses were classified on the basis of the host organism and the kind of disease they caused. Due to the overlap in various areas (i.e., the same virus has more than one host), it became necessary to classify viruses using a system that also includes the nature of the individual virus particle.

Objective 1. Relate the use of viral family subgroups.
Objective 2. Explain the use of genera.

A. What are the two superfamilies of animal viruses, and into how many families can each be further divided?

Discuss the naming of a viral family.

List the characteristics used for placement of a virus in a particular family.

B.   What is the basis for assigning viruses genus status?

Discuss the naming of viral genera.

Standardized species names are widely accepted. True/False

IV. MODES OF VIRAL MULTIPLICATION

Concept: Viruses as obligate parasites must appropriate the synthetic and genetic machinery of host cells for multiplication.

Objective 1.   Compare and contrast the events involved in the multiplication cycle of a bacteriophage and an animal virus (both of which demonstrate host specificity).

Objective 2.   Discuss the effects of animal viral infections on host cells.

Objective 3.   Describe techniques for cultivating and identifying animal viruses.

A.   Summarize each event in the multiplication cycle of a bacteriophage:

adsorption—

penetration—

replication—

assembly (maturation)—

release (lytic cycle)—

Not all bacteriophages complete the lytic cycle. Describe the alternative—lysogeny.

Summarize each event in the multiplication cycle of an animal virus:

adsorption—

penetration—

uncoating—

replication—

assembly—

release—

B. Define cytopathic effect.

List some common CPE.

Give some examples of persistent viral infections.

Explain oncogenic viruses and cell transformation.

C. List the primary purposes of viral cultivation in a medical setting.

Describe two *in vivo* methods for viral cultivation.

Describe an *in vitro* method for viral cultivation.

Differentiate between primary and continuous cell cultures.

Areas where virus-infected cells have been destroyed will show clearing in an agar culture called _____.

V. MEDICAL IMPORTANCE OF VIRUSES

Concept: Viruses are the most common cause of acute infections that do not result in hospitalization.

Objective 1. Discuss the medical importance (detection, control, and treatment) of viral infections.

A. Indicate and explain the three methods used to identify viruses.

Name two antiviral drugs, and indicate how they affect viral control.

VI. SELF-TEST

1. Pasteur proposed the term *virus,* which is Latin for
   a. small thing.
   b. living thing.
   c. poison.
   d. invisible thing.
   e. infectious agent.

2. Filterable viruses are
   a. smaller than bacteria.
   b. larger than bacteria.
   c. larger than protozoans.
   d. larger than yeast.
   e. larger than molds.

3. Viruses are visible through a
   a. fluorescent microscope.
   b. dark-field microscope.
   c. light microscope.
   d. electron microscope.
   e. phase-contrast microscope.

4. The nucleocapsid is composed of
   a. nucleic acid and carbohydrate.
   b. nucleic acid and protein.
   c. nucleic acid and lipid.
   d. nucleic acid only.
   e. none of the above.

5. Virus genera are assigned a name comprised of a Latin root followed by -viridae.
   a. True
   b. False

6. Maturation of a viral particle involves the
   a. recognition process between the virus and host cell, which results in virus attachment to the host cell.
   b. entrance of the virion into the host cell.
   c. expression of the viral genome at the expense of the host's synthetic equipment.
   d. infectious viral particle's escape from the host cell.
   e. assembly of viral parts into the whole intact virions.

7. Human cells resist infection with the canine hepatitis virus, and dog cells are not naturally invaded by human hepatitis A virus due to a resistant cell that blocks the adsorption of the virus.
   a. True
   b. False

8. Cytopathic effects of viruses on host cells include
   a. disorientation of individual cells.
   b. gross changes in size and/or shape of the cells.
   c. intracellular changes such as inclusion bodies forming within the cell.
   d. all of the above.
   e. none of the above.

9. Viral propagation may be carried out
   a. in the absence of host cells.
   b. on artificial media.
   c. within embryonated duck eggs.
   d. in all of the above.
   e. in none of the above.

10. All of the following are used to prevent or treat viral infections *except*
    a. acyclovir.
    b. azidothymidine.
    c. interferon.
    d. vaccines.
    e. antibiotics.

11. The first rabies vaccine was developed by
    a. Ivanovski.
    b. Pasteur.
    c. Loeffler.
    d. Frosch.
    e. Beijerinck.

12. A convenient and relatively useful substitute host for many animal viruses is
    a. plant tissue cultures.
    b. plant leaves.
    c. bacterial cultures.
    d. bird embryos.
    e. all of the above.

13. Which of the following is not found in all viruses?
    a. nucleic acid
    b. protein
    c. an envelope
    d. enzymes
    e. a capsid

14. The useful method of diagnosing viral diseases is
    a. administration of broad spectrum antibiotics.
    b. isolation of the virus and study of its structure.
    c. isolation and cultivation of the virus in cell culture.
    d. evaluation of the overall symptoms and signs.
    e. all of the above.

15. The only really effective defense currently available against viral infections is
    a. federal legislation.
    b. antibiotics.
    c. vaccination.
    d. education.
    e. all of the above.

16. Change in the microscopic appearance of a host cell is called
    a. exocytosis.
    b. cytopathic effect.
    c. lysogenic effect.
    d. lysis.
    e. phagocytosis.

17. The release of animal viruses from their host occurs in
    a. exocytosis.
    b. endocytosis.
    c. maturation.
    d. eclipse.
    e. lysis.

18. All viruses are obligate intracellular parasites.
    a. True
    b. False

19. Some viruses can contain both DNA and RNA.
    a. True
    b. False

20. Viruses cannot be cultured in living cells, only in artificial media.
    a. True
    b. False

7 Elements of Microbial Nutrition, Ecology, and Growth

OVERVIEW

Microorganisms grow under various conditions involving nutrient and energy sources, temperature, moisture, gaseous environment, osmotic pressure, pH, presence or absence of light or radiation, and presence of other organisms. Changes in any or all of these conditions can alter the growth pattern of the microorganism. The study of microbial growth patterns involves determining generation times and normal growth curves.

I. INTRODUCTION

Concept: Microbes are able to adapt to a wide variety of habitats.

II. MICROBIAL NUTRITION

Concept: Among the factors affecting microbial growth are nutrition and energy source.

> **Objective 1.** Demonstrate that essential nutrients vary greatly from microbe to microbe.
> **Objective 2.** Correlate how sources of essential nutrients may overlap, with many components furnishing more than one given element.
> **Objective 3.** Define microbial nutritional types with respect to carbon and energy sources.

A. Essential nutrients do not vary greatly from microbe to microbe. Variation occurs in the ultimate source of a particular element, its chemical form, and how much of it the microbe needs. True/False

Define **macronutrients,** including their principal roles and examples.

Define **micronutrients,** including their principal roles and examples.

Describe and give examples of **inorganic nutrients.**

Describe and give examples of **organic nutrients.**

B.   Complete the chart.

Nutrient	Function in the cell	Source
carbon (heterotrophs)		
carbon (autotrophs)		
nitrogen		
oxygen		
hydrogen		
phosphorus		
sulfur		

Any organic compound that must be obtained from the environment (cannot be synthesized by an organism) is called an _____ _____.

C.   Complete the chart.

	Carbon source	Energy source	Microbial example
photoautotroph			
chemoautotroph			
chemoheterotroph (saprobe)			
chemoheterotroph (parasite)			

III. TRANSPORT MECHANISMS FOR NUTRIENT ABSORPTION

Concept: Nutrients move into the cell by the processes of both passive and active transport.

Objective 1. Describe various transport mechanisms used in microbial absorption of nutrients.

A.   List and define three general types of passive transport.

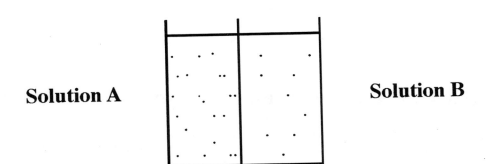

Solution A   **Solution B**

Solution A is separated from solution B by a selectively permeable membrane.

What is the tonicity of solution A compared to solution B?

In which direction will osmosis occur?

Compare and contrast diffusion and facilitated diffusion.

List the features inherent in active transport systems.

Describe two forms of endocytosis (bulk transport):

phagocytosis—

pinocytosis—

IV. ENVIRONMENTAL FACTORS THAT INFLUENCE MICROBES

Concept: Environmental factors such as temperature, gases, pH, radiation, moisture, and osmotic and hydrostatic pressures affect microbial cells as demonstrated by their continued growth, death, or mere tolerance of given conditions.

Objective 1. Describe the various temperature requirements of microbes.
Objective 2. Describe the various gas requirements of microbes.
Objective 3. Give an overview of the major types of microbial interactions.

A. Complete the chart.

Microbe	Temperature range	Optimum temperature	Habitat
psychrophile			
mesophile			
thermophile			

B. List three gases that influence microbial growth.

With respect to oxygen requirements, characterize:

aerobes—

facultative anaerobes—

microaerophiles—

anaerobes—

C. Define:

symbiosis—

44

commensalism—

parasitism—

synergism—

antagonism—

V. THE STUDY OF MICROBIAL GROWTH

Concept: Microbial growth involves both an increase in the number of cells in a population as well as an increase in the size of a single cell.

Objective 1. Correlate bacterial binary fission with generation time.
Objective 2. Describe the normal bacterial population growth curve.
Objective 3. Indicate methods of enumerating bacteria and measuring bacterial growth.

A. Binary (transverse) fission is the process whereby the parent cell enlarges, chromosomes duplicate, and a septum forms to divide the cell into four daughter cells. True/False

An organism X with a generation time of 10 minutes colonizes an area. Calculate the number of organism X cells found in the area after 1½ hours.

B. What is meant by a bacterial culture being closed?

Characterize each of the four phases of the bacterial growth curve.

C. What does the turbidity of a bacterial culture indicate?

Discuss how bacterial cells are enumerated.

VI. SELF-TEST

1. About 96% of the cell is composed of
   a. carbon, hydrogen, nitrogen, oxygen, phosphorus, sulfur.
   b. chlorine, hydrogen, nitrogen, oxygen, phosphorus, sulfur.
   c. chlorine, helium, nitrogen, oxygen, phosphorus, sulfur.
   d. chlorine, helium, nickel, oxygen, phosphorus, sulfur.
   e. carbon, hydrogen, nitrogen, oxygen, potassium, sulfur.

2. Potassium is an essential mineral ion. It is
   a. an important component of the cytochrome pigments.
   b. a participant in the energetics of the cell.
   c. a stabilizer of the cell wall.
   d. essential to protein synthesis.
   e. a component of chlorophyll.

3. Microbes that will not grow without added growth factors, complex nutrients, or other conditions are termed
   a. heterotrophic.
   b. autotrophic.
   c. fastidious.
   d. aerobic.
   e. thermophilic.

4. Growth factors include
   a. amino acids.
   b. vitamins.
   c. nucleotides.
   d. all of the above.
   e. none of the above.

5. Microbes are so immensely adaptable that they have proliferated into every type of habitat and niche.
   a. True
   b. False

6. A membrane that allows free movement of water but blocks the movement of larger molecules is
   a. permeable.
   b. selectively permeable.
   c. impermeable.

7. A solution equal in concentration to the cell's internal environment is
   a. hypotonic.
   b. hypertonic.
   c. isotonic.

8. The optimum pH range for most human pathogens is
   a. 4.5 to 5.5.
   b. 5.5 to 6.5.
   c. 6.5 to 7.5.
   d. 7.5 to 8.5.
   e. 8.5 to 9.5.

9. Halophiles (osmophiles) live in solutions that are
   a. hypotonic.
   b. hypertonic.
   c. isotonic.

10. Normal flora participate in what type of relationship(s) with their human hosts?
    a. symbiotic
    b. synergistic
    c. commensalistic
    d. parasitic
    e. all of the above

11. If a cell is placed in a medium containing a higher glucose concentration than is found inside the cell
    a. glucose will move out of the cell by osmosis.
    b. glucose will move into the cell by osmosis.
    c. water will move out of the cell by osmosis.
    d. water will move into the cell by osmosis.
    e. nothing will happen with respect to osmosis.

12. The most abundant element in a bacterial cell is
    a. carbon.
    b. oxygen.
    c. nitrogen.
    d. carbohydrate.
    e. protein.

13. During which growth phase is a gram positive bacteria most susceptible to penicillin?
    a. lag phase
    b. log growth phase
    c. death phase
    d. stationary phase
    e. all phases are equally susceptible

14. An experiment began with 6 cells and ended with 192 cells. How many generations did the cells go through?
    a. 48
    b. 24
    c. 6
    d. 5
    e. 4

15. Which of the following is mismatched?
    a. thermophile—growth at 37 degrees Celsius
    b. mesophile—growth at 25 degrees Celsius
    c. psychrophile—growth at 10 degrees Celsius
    d. aerotolerant—an anaerobe that may survive in atmospheric oxygen
    e. facultative anaerobe—prefers to grow in atmospheric oxygen, but may grow without atmospheric oxygen

Matching.
16. _____ diffusion
17. _____ osmosis
18. _____ active transport
19. _____ phagocytosis
20. _____ pinocytosis

a. low to high concentration
b. high to low concentration
c. bacteria forms oil vesicle
d. water follows salt
e. white blood cell engulfs bacterium

8 Microbial Metabolism: The Chemical Crossroads of Life

OVERVIEW

Metabolism is cyclical, including all the biochemical, self-regulating, interdependent, enzymatically controlled reactions occurring within the cell. Those reactions that are anabolic or synthetic require energy, while those reactions that are catabolic or degradative release energy. Thus, the energy from the catabolic reactions drives the anabolic reactions.

I.   INTRODUCTION

Concept: Studies of microbial metabolism have helped in the identification of pathogens, production of hormones, vitamins, and antibiotics, as well as in the understanding of human cell physiology.

II.   THE METABOLISM OF MICROBES

Concept: An understanding of microbial metabolic processes is important because they affect the success of drug therapy, are used to identify bacteria, and are relied upon to produce an ever-increasing array of products.

Objective 1.   Contrast anabolism and catabolism, which are the two general categories for the thousands of different reactions involved in metabolism.
Objective 2.   Define enzyme and indicate how an enzyme functions.
Objective 3.   Discuss the structure of an enzyme.
Objective 4.   Describe enzyme-substrate interactions.
Objective 5.   Explain the significance of cofactors and coenzymes.
Objective 6.   Describe the various types of reactions catalyzed by enzymes.
Objective 7.   Identify environmental conditions that affect enzyme activity, and explain denaturation.
Objective 8.   Discuss the control of enzymes.

A.   Matching.

____ synthesis
____ requires the input of energy
____ degradation
____ forms larger molecules from smaller units
____ converts larger molecules into smaller
       components
____ often produces energy

a.   anabolism
b.   catabolism

B.   What are enzyme catalysts?

Why are enzymes necessary to sustain life?

An enzyme becomes physically attached to the substrate and participates directly in bonding. It does not become a part of the product(s), is not used up by the reaction, and can function continuously. True/False

C.   Contrast a simple enzyme with a conjugated enzyme.

A _____ is a combination of an apoenzyme and cofactor or coenzyme.

D.   Describe the "lock-and-key" concept as it applies to enzyme and substrate interactions.

E.   Recall the function(s) of metallic cofactors.

Describe the function of a coenzyme.

A diet without _____ would be incomplete, since these organic compounds are necessary as, or as a part of, coenzymes.

F.   Identify the type of reaction illustrated in each of the following examples:

_____   The reaction of two monosaccharides joining together requires energy and produces a disaccharide and a molecule of water.

_____   The dissolution of a disaccharide requires the input of a molecule of water and results in two monosaccharides.

_____   In the process of breaking glucose down into two pyruvic acid molecules, hydrogen atoms are removed from glucose (glucose loses electrons) and are added to NAD (NAD gains electrons).

G. Name three environmental conditions that affect enzyme function.

Define denaturation.

List some denaturing agents.

H. Distinguish between various direct controls on the behavior of enzymes:

competitive inhibition—

negative feedback—

feedback inhibition—

What happens to enzymes in the cell?

Contrast feedback repression and enzyme induction.

III. THE PURSUIT AND UTILIZATION OF ENERGY

Concept: The ultimate source of energy is the sun, but only chemical energy operates the major cell processes of biosynthesis, movement, transport, and growth.

Objective 1. Summarize how a cell converts potential energy into kinetic energy.
Objective 2. Describe biological oxidation and reduction.
Objective 3. Discuss the structure of ATP as it relates to function.

A. Define potential and kinetic energy.

Do cells "create" energy? Explain your answer.

B. Label the reaction as to which compound is being oxidized and which compou

Compound X donates an electron to Compound Y

[Compound X - (e-) → (e-) + Compound Y]

Redox reactions release kinetic energy used for phosphorylation. What does phosphoı ⸜ involve?

Relate how the cell handles electrons as part of an atom such as hydrogen.

Discuss the function of electron carriers.

List common redox carriers.

Give the final electron acceptor for:

aerobes—

anaerobes—

C. Describe the molecular structure of ATP.

Explain the mechanism by which ATP releases a burst of energy.

ATP expenditures must inevitably be followed by ATP regeneration. Indicate which of the following types of reactions *expends* ATP. Indicate which of the following types of reactions *regenerates* ATP.

catabolic reactions—

anabolic reactions—

___ substrate level phosphorylation	a. energy is released from a series of redox reactions occurring during the final phase of the respiratory pathway
___ oxidative phosphorylation	
___ photophosphorylation	
	b. energy is released directly from a substrate in a reaction to ADP
	c. ATP energy is formed through a series of sunlight-driven reactions

IV. PATHWAYS OF BIOENERGETICS

Concept: The complexity of life's total metabolic scheme is staggering, with interdependent and interconnected pathways allowing anabolism and catabolism to proceed simultaneously.

Objective 1. Relate the pathways involved in the catabolism of fuels to release energy.
Objective 2. Discuss the various energy strategies used by microorganisms.
Objective 3. Detail the anaerobic process of glycolysis.
Objective 4. Discuss the ways various organisms handle pyruvic acid.
Objective 5. Summarize the process of aerobic respiration.
Objective 6. Summarize the process of anaerobic respiration.
Objective 7. Summarize the process of fermentation.

A. List three pathways used in the catabolism of fuels resulting in the release of energy.

B. Distinguish between the various processes used and the different electron acceptors (final hydrogen acceptors) involved as microbes process nutrients.

aerobic respiration—

anaerobic respiration—

fermentation—

C. Identify the compound indicated by the question marks on the diagram of glycolysis.*

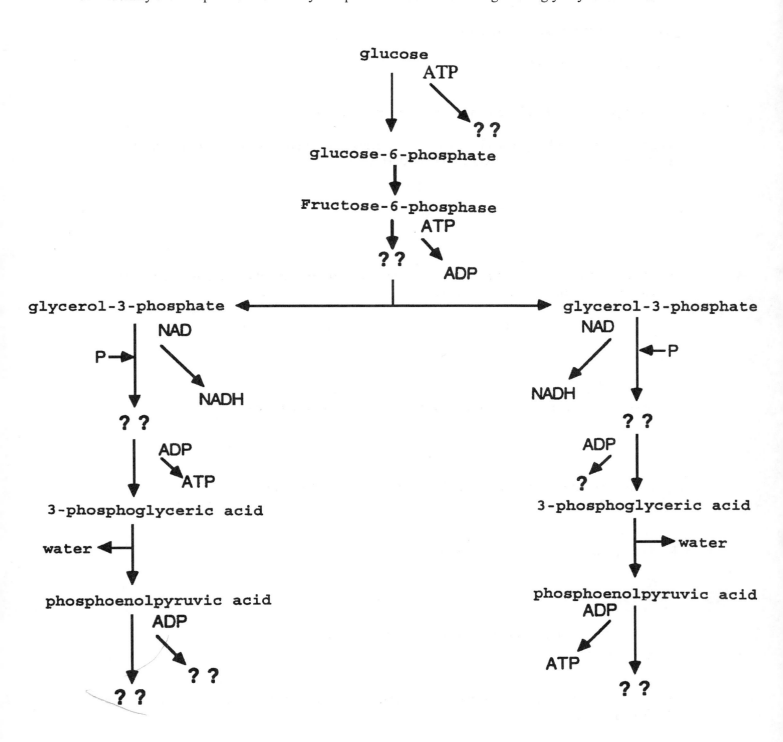

*Indicate where substrate phosphorylation occurs.

D. What further processing of pyruvic acid occurs:

in aerobic organisms and some anaerobes?

in facultative anaerobes?

E. The continuation of aerobic respiration is a two phase process.

Summarize the tricarboxylic acid cycle (TCA) in terms of what goes into the series of reactions, and what comes out (i.e. carbon dioxide, ATP, NADH, etc.).

Summarize the respiratory chain in terms of what goes into the series of carriers, the linear sequence of reduction/oxidation, and the end result.

The electron transport chain is an example of what type of phosphorylation?

Where is the electron transport system located in procaryotes? in eucaryotes?

Review the significance of cytochrome oxidase.

F. Compare and contrast anaerobic respiration to aerobic respiration.

G. Indicate the terminal electron acceptor in the fermentation (incomplete oxidation) of glucose in the absence of oxygen.

List some products of the fermentation of pyruvic acid.

V. BIOSYNTHESIS AND THE CROSSING PATHWAYS OF METABOLISM

Concept: Anabolic functions within the cell include amphibolic pathways, the synthesis of simple molecules, and the synthesis of macromolecules.

Objective 1. Demonstrate branch points and crossroads (amphibolic pathways) of several metabolic pathways.
Objective 2. Discuss the relationship between catabolic pathways and biosynthesis.

A. Complete the chart.

Compound	Pathway diverted from	Precursor for
glyceraldehyde-3-phosphate		
pyruvic acid (pyruvate)		
acetyl group		
oxaloacetate		
α-ketoglutarate		

B. Explain how the catabolic pathways of glycolysis and oxidative phosphorylation contribute to the biosynthesis of proteins, nucleic acids, lipids, and glycogen.

Microorganisms are able to synthesize all of their own building blocks used in the formation of macromolecules. True/False

Synthesis of macromolecules involve the formation of bonds by specialized anabolic _____ and the expenditure of _____.

VI. SELF-TEST

1. Characteristics of enzymes include all *except* they
   a. are protein catalysts to speed up the rate of cellular reactions.
   b. are not used up or permanently changed by the reaction.
   c. are unique with respect to shape, specificity, and function.
   d. work slowly.
   e. need lower energy of activation for chemical reactions.

2. Bonds between an enzyme and substrate are strong and irreversible.
   a. True
   b. False

3. All of the following are enzymes *except*
   a. lactose.
   b. dehydrogenase.
   c. lipase.
   d. peptidase.
   e. catalase.

4. An enzyme not constantly present, but produced only when its substrate is present is called
   a. an exoenzyme.
   b. an endoenzyme.
   c. an induced enzyme.
   d. a constitutive enzyme.
   e. none of the above.

5. Metabolic reactions are multi-step series or pathways, each step catalyzed by an enzyme.
   a. True
   b. False

6. Which type of organism converts solar energy through photosynthesis into the chemical energy which subsequently becomes a source of energy for other living things?
   a. chemoheterotroph
   b. chemoautotroph
   c. photoheterotroph
   d. photoautotroph
   e. none of the above

7. In aerobic respiration, glucose is the electron donor and _____ is the final electron acceptor.
   a. carbon
   b. hydrogen
   c. oxygen
   d. nitrogen
   e. helium

8. Fermentation, though inefficient, permits microbial independence from molecular carbon and allows adaptation to variations in availability of carbon.
   a. True
   b. False

9. Aerobic respiration occurs in the _____ of eucaryotic cells and in the _____ of bacteria.
   a. nucleus, ribosomes
   b. nucleus, cytoplasm
   c. cytoplasm, cytoplasm
   d. cytoplasm, mitochondria
   e. mitochondria, cytoplasm

10. Aerobic respiration of one glucose molecule yields
    a. 2 ATP.
    b. 4 ATP.
    c. 36 ATP.
    d. 38 ATP.
    e. 40 ATP.

11. Most coenzymes are
    a. ions.
    b. vitamins.
    c. proteins.
    d. carbohydrates.
    e. nucleic acids.

12. Glycolysis produces a net total of ____ ATP molecules.
    a. 1
    b. 2
    c. 3
    d. 4
    e. 38

13. In aerobic respiration, glucose is the electron donor and what is the final electron acceptor?
    a. carbon
    b. hydrogen
    c. oxygen
    d. nitrogen
    e. helium

14. ATP contains ribose, phosphate, and _____.
    a. cytosine
    b. uracil
    c. thymine
    d. guanine
    e. adenine

15. The citric acid cycle occurs in the _____ of procaryotes.
    a. cell wall
    b. cell membrane
    c. cytoplasm
    d. nucleoid
    e. mitochondrion

16. Catabolism, also called biosynthesis, results in synthesis of cell molecules and structures.
    a. True
    b. False

17. In oxidation/reduction reactions, the compound that loses electrons is
    a. oxidized.
    b. reduced.
    c. neutralized.
    d. stabilized.
    e. revitalized.

18. In negative feedback control of a metabolic process, the process is inhibited by the product.
    a. True
    b. False

19. _____ energy can be directed toward synthesis, movement, and growth.
    a. Potential
    b. Kinetic

20. Formation of ATP can occur through
    a. substrate-level phosphorylation.
    b. oxidative phosphorylation.
    c. photophosphorylation.
    d. all of the above.
    e. none of the above.

9 Microbial Genetics

OVERVIEW

Microbes, both procaryotic and eucaryotic cells, contain DNA—the genetic material that must by copied prior to cell division. Sections of DNA code for proteins necessary for the livelihood of the cell. DNA can mutate as well as be transferred from one cell to another. The study of the properties of microbial DNA and inheritance is called microbial genetics.

I. INTRODUCTION TO GENETICS AND GENES: UNLOCKING THE SECRETS OF HEREDITY

Concept: Microbial genetics, the study of heredity, exists on the cellular and molecular levels.

Objective 1. Illustrate the significance of a genome, including the chromosomes and genes that make up the genome.

Objective 2. Describe in detail the structure of deoxyribonucleic acid (DNA).

Objective 3. Summarize the replication of DNA.

A. Define genome.

Describe the form in which a genome exists.

Describe the structure of a chromosome.

Contrast eucaryotic and bacterial chromosomes.

Define gene.

What substances do genes code for?

List the characteristics of *E. coli* that make this organism a good working model for genetics studies.

B. Recall the general structure of DNA. Simplified, DNA appears to be a twisted ladder.

The sides of the ladder are repeating units of _____ and
_____. The rungs of the ladder are nitrogenous bases covalently bonded to
the sugars making up the sides of the ladder.

Discuss the specific pairing of purines and pyrimidines including the bond connecting each pair.

Give the complementary strand of DNA for GGCGTTAGGAAT.

C. Explain the purpose of DNA replication.

List the steps of DNA replication.

Describe semiconservative replication and discuss its significance.

II. APPLICATIONS OF THE DNA CODE: TRANSCRIPTION AND TRANSLATION

Concept: DNA does not directly carry out cell processes; rather, its stored information is conveyed to
other molecules that carry out its instructions.

  Objective 1. Explain the connection between genes and proteins.
  Objective 2. Discuss transcription.
  Objective 3. Discuss translation.
  Objective 4. Describe the basic differences between procaryotic and eucaryotic gene expression.
  Objective 5. Describe replication, transcription, and translation of viruses.

A. List the three basic categories of genes.

Discuss triplets and their function in protein synthesis.

Characterize messenger RNA (mRNA), made up of codons.

Characterize transfer RNA (tRNA), made up of anticodons.

B. In transcription, DNA becomes untwisted and separates into two strands to expose the message that is copied onto an mRNA molecule. The resulting mRNA is a replica of the _____ strand of DNA.

Propose the mRNA strand transcribed from the DNA strand GGCGTTAGGAAT.

Describe the stages of transcription:

initiation—

elongation—

termination—

C. Describe the stages of translation:

initiation—

elongation—

termination—

protein folding and processing—

Translate the amino acids as they are coded for in the mRNA strand CCGCAAUCCUUA.

Explain the completion of protein synthesis.

D. Contrast gene expression in procaryotic and eucaryotic cells.

E. Discuss reverse transcriptase as it occurs with the retrovirus HIV.

III. GENETIC REGULATION OF PROTEIN SYNTHESIS AND METABOLISM

Concept: Regulation of genes generally occurs at the level of transcription.

Objective 1. Describe an operon as it affects gene control.
Objective 2. Distinguish between inducible and repressible operons.

A. Define operon.

What roles do the regulator operator and promoter genes play in bacterial gene control?

B. List the segments of DNA composing an inducible operon.

What is the significance of the inducible operon normally functioning in the *off* mode?

State the function of the repressible operon.

What is the significance of the repressible operon normally functioning in the *on* mode?

IV. CHANGES IN THE GENETIC CODE: MUTATIONS AND INTERMICROBIAL EXCHANGE AND RECOMBINATION

Concept: A mutation is an alteration in the base sequence of DNA.

Objective 1. Discuss spontaneous and induced mutations.
Objective 2. Describe the varieties of mutations and their outcomes.
Objective 3. Explain the Ames test for mutagenesis.
Objective 4. Discuss microbial genetic recombination.

A. Define:

spontaneous mutations— *P.g 280 (causes of Mutation)*
random change in DNA arising from mistakes in replication
or the detrimental effect of natural background radiation -
induced mutations—
results from exposure to mutagen (physical or chemical agents)

List and relate the mode of action of the physical agents that alter DNA.

radiation
The overall effect of radiation depends on its length & intensity

high energy gamma rays) produce reactive free radical
X - rays . - also causes Cancer
U - V (breaks bonds between Pyrimidines) causes leukemia
nuclear radiation

The overall effects of radiation depend upon _____ *Intensity of radiation .* and _____ *Length*

P.g 281 Categories of Mutation

B. Relate what happens to the DNA genetic code when:

a point mutation occurs— *Involves the addition, deletion, or substitution of new bases.*

pg 282
a missense mutation occurs— *where a change of code that leads to placement of different amino acid can cause one of following: ①create a faulty non-functional protein, ② Produce a different but functional protein, ③ cause no significant alteration in Protein function.*

a nonsense mutation occurs— *changes a normal codon into a stop codon that doesn't code for an amino acid and stops the production of protein whenever it occurs.*

62

What repair processes exist for damaged or mutated DNA? *(Repair Mutatn Pg 283)*

C. Name and describe the indicator organism for the Ames test. *Pg 284*

When is an Ames test agent considered a mutagen? *Pg 284*

D. Summarize the modes of microbial genetic exchange: *Transfer & Recombnatn 285*

conjugation—

transformation—

transduction—

Discuss the significance of plasmids. *285 & 287*

Explain transposons, or "jumping genes." *Transposon Pg 290*

Contrast the beneficial and adverse effects of transposons. *Pg 290*

V. SELF-TEST

1. The length of the DNA is proportional to the size of the cell, short enough to fit within even the smallest cell.
   a. True
   b. False

2. In DNA, adenine pairs with
   a. adenine.
   b. guanine.
   c. thymine.
   d. cytosine.
   e. none of the above.

3. Mistakes in the base sequences of the growing DNA chain during replication either are corrected or become mutations.
   a. True
   b. False

4. The sum total of an organism's structural genes constitutes its
   a. appearance.
   b. phenotype.
   c. function.
   d. genotype.
   e. none of the above.

5. Transcription is the process of copying the DNA code to a strand of
   a. DNA.
   b. messenger RNA (mRNA).
   c. transfer RNA (tRNA).
   d. ribosomal RNA (rRNA).
   e. none of the above.

6. Translation occurs in the
   a. nucleus.
   b. cytoplasm.
   c. mitochondria.
   d. plasma membrane.
   e. ribosomes.

7. Antibiotics inhibit the growth of infectious agents by affecting
   a. transcription.
   b. translation.
   c. replication.
   d. a and b.
   e. a and c.

8. Chemicals capable of mutating bacterial DNA do not usually cause a similar mutation in mammalian cells.
   a. True
   b. False

9. Mutations are permanent and heritable.
   a. True
   b. False

10. The properties of bacteria that influence recombination are:
    a. genetic material found solely in one chromosome.
    b. possession of extrachromosomal DNA.
    c. ability to interchange genes without disruption.
    d. a and b.
    e. b and c.

11. The two strands of DNA are held together by
    a. carbon bonds.
    b. phosphate bonds.
    c. double bonds.
    d. disulfide linkages.
    e. hydrogen bonds.

12. The semiconservative replication of DNA means that
    a. DNA is a double helix.
    b. the two new DNA molecules will be different from the original DNA molecule.
    c. one of the new DNA molecules will contain two new strands of DNA, while the other contains both old strands.
    d. the two new molecules of DNA will contain uracil instead of thymine.
    e. the two new molecules of DNA will each have one old strand and one new strand, and be identical to the original DNA molecule.

13. A gene is considered to code for a
    a. trait.
    b. cell division.
    c. tissue type.
    d. protein.
    e. phenotypic structure.

14. Which of these is not part of DNA?
    a. deoxyribose
    b. phosphate
    c. thymine
    d. cytosine
    e. uracil

15. In RNA, adenine can form a base pair with
    a. thymine.
    b. guanine.
    c. uracil.
    d. cytosine.
    e. adenine.

16. The anticodon for mRNA UGC is
    a. AGC.
    b. ACG.
    c. TGC.
    d. TCG.
    e. UGC.

17. The sugar in DNA is
    a. ribose.
    b. deoxyribose.
    c. glucose.
    d. dextrose.
    e. lactose.

18. If a protein is coded for 450 bases, how many amino acids make up the protein?
    a. 900
    b. 450
    c. 300
    d. 150
    e. 100

19. The best definition of a genome is
    a. inheritance.
    b. the sum total of all the genetic material in the cell.
    c. the site on the chromosome providing information for a certain cell function.
    d. the extrachromosomal DNA.
    e. a trait.

20. The codon for a DNA section with ACG is
    a. ACG.
    b. GCA.
    c. UCG.
    d. TGC.
    e. UGC.

10   Genetic Engineering: A Revolution in Molecular Biology

OVERVIEW

Scientists are able to manipulate, alter, and analyze genetic material. This knowledge is both beneficial and controversial. Benefits include production of pharmaceuticals, improvement of crops and foods, and gene therapy in the treatment of disease. Controversial issues include the accuracy of DNA fingerprinting evidence in court and the genetic alteration of human gametes.

I.   INTRODUCTION

Concept: Microbial genetic material can be manipulated, altered, and analyzed.

II.   TOOLS AND TECHNIQUES OF GENETIC ENGINEERING

Concept: Highly sophisticated laboratory tools and techniques show actual DNA patterns.

> **Objective 1.**   Explain the annealing of DNA.
> **Objective 2.**   Describe the use of enzymes in the study of DNA.
> **Objective 3.**   Discuss the visualization of DNA.
> **Objective 4.**   Detail the use of gene probes and production of blots to demonstrate hybridization.
> **Objective 5.**   Discuss the amplification of DNA fragments by the polymerase chain reaction (PCR).

A.   What happens to the structure of DNA when it is heated to temperatures just below boiling?

What happens to the structure of DNA when it is slowly cooled following heating?

B.   List the enzymes and their specific application(s) in the study of DNA.

C.   Describe the process of gel electrophoresis.

Indicate the use(s) of gel electrophoresis.

D. Define:

hybrid—

gene probe—

Contrast the Southern and Northern blots.

How are gene probes used to diagnose disease?

List some of the organisms for which probes are available.

E. Outline the three steps that cycle repeatedly during polymerase chain reactions.

Can PCR be used to analyze RNA? If so, how? If not, why?

Indicate some of the problems with PCR.

III. METHODS IN RECOMBINANT DNA TECHNOLOGY: HOW TO IMITATE NATURE

Concept: Recombinant DNA technology is readily accomplished in bacteria and can be used to mass-produce hormones, enzymes, vaccine, and other substances difficult to industrially synthesize.

Objective 1. Describe the process of making a genetic clone.

A. Define clone.

Explain in detail what is involved in cloning.

Why are yeast plasmids (YACs) better cloning vectors than bacterial plasmids?

What characteristics of *Escherichia coli,* the traditional cloning host, make it undesirable?

IV. BIOCHEMICAL PRODUCTS OF RECOMBINANT DNA TECHNOLOGY RECOMBINANT ORGANISMS: HOW TO IMPROVE ON NATURE

Concept: Applications of genetic engineering include: bioengineered products, gene therapy and genetic medicines, and genomic mapping and analysis.

Objective 1. Discuss the use of recombinant DNA technology by pharmaceutical companies to manufacture medications.
Objective 2. Identify the process of artificially introducing foreign genes into organisms and the organism produced.
Objective 3. Discuss specific examples of modified microbes, plants, and animals.
Objective 4. Discuss two strategies for gene therapy.
Objective 5. Explain the difficulty in accomplishing gene therapy.
Objective 6. Describe the use of genetic drugs in bypassing the problem gene and protein.
Objective 7. Explain the practical uses of genetic mapping.

A. List and describe the use of several products manufactured as a result of recombinant DNA technology.

B. Define:

transfection—

transgenic—

68

C. Indicate an agricultural use of recombinant microbes.

What agency monitors the release of these recombinant microbes?

Indicate a plant that has been transfected and the benefit derived from the recombination.

Describe the most effective way to insert genes into animals.

D. Contrast *ex vivo* and *in vivo* strategies for gene therapy.

E. List the problems hampering gene therapy.

F. What is an antisense strand of nucleic acid?

Indicate two effects of cellular uptake of antisense DNA.

List several diseases amenable to antisense DNA therapy.

What does triplex DNA do to cell cultures?

G. Choose one application of genetic mapping and thoroughly discuss its use.

V. SELF-TEST

1. Sequencers are machines that read the precise order of the
    a. genes.
    b. genome.
    c. nucleotides in DNA fragments.
    d. amino acids in a protein.
    e. none of the above.

2. Techniques to analyze DNA and RNA may be limited by the small amounts of test nucleic acid available.
    a. True
    b. False

3. Gene cloning and isolation can be very laborious, and unfortunately cannot be maintained in the cloning host and vector for an extended period of time.
    a. True
    b. False

4. Plasmids are excellent cloning vectors because they are
    a. small.
    b. well characterized.
    c. easy to manipulate.
    d. transferred into appropriate host cells through transformation.
    e. all of the above.

5. Transgenic "designer" organisms can be patented.
    a. True
    b. False

6. Which of the following most closely express human genes in organs and organ systems that are very similar to humans?
    a. transgenic microbes
    b. transgenic plants
    c. transgenic animals
    d. a and c
    e. none of the above

7. The rate of productive transfection by viruses to the target cells in gene therapy is
    a. extremely high (>90%).
    b. very high (about 70%).
    c. moderate (about 45%).
    d. very low (about 10%).
    e. extremely low (<1%).

8. Early gene treatment in both adenosine deaminase (ADA) deficiency and cystic fibrosis is
    a. permanent.
    b. impermanent.
    c. long-lasting.
    d. ineffective in reducing the severity of disease.
    e. none of the above.

9. Gene therapy could be a boon for persons with a number of multiple-gene defects.
    a. True
    b. False

10. "Junk DNA" does not code for a protein, but does carry important support information.
    a. True
    b. False

11. In gel electrophoresis, samples are placed in wells in a soft gel agar and subjected to an electric current. Flow of electricity from the negative pole to the positive pole causes the DNA pieces to migrate toward the negative pole.
    a. True
    b. False

12. The enzyme reverse transcriptase provides a tool for making copy DNA (cDNA) from
    a. RNA.
    b. mRNA.
    c. tRNA.
    d. rRNA.
    e. all of the above.

13. Polymerase chain reaction (PCR) amplifies DNA, increasing the amount of DNA in a sample.
    a. True
    b. False

14. Bioengineered hormones are less expensive and less effective than similar substances derived from animals.
    a. True
    b. False

15. How are endonucleases named?
    a. for a gene
    b. for the persons who discovered them
    c. in numerical order of their discovery
    d. by combining the first letter of the bacterial genus, the first two letters of the species, and the endonuclease number
    e. none of the above

16. Two different nucleic acids can _____ by uniting at their complementary sites, a property that has been the inspiration for gene probes.
    a. visualize
    b. standardize
    c. hybridize
    d. combine
    e. synthesize

17. The PCR technique operates by repetitive cycling of three basic steps
    a. denaturation, priming, and extension.
    b. priming, denaturation, and extension.
    c. denaturation, amplification, and extension.
    d. priming, amplification, and extension.
    e. none of the above.

18. Characteristics of cloning vectors include
    a. capable of carrying a significant piece of the donor DNA.
    b. readily accepted by the cloning host.
    c. small, well characterized, and easy to manipulate.
    d. able to carry huge genome sequences.
    e. all of the above.

19. The traditional cloning host and the one still used in most experiments is
    a. *Escherichia coli.*
    b. *Saccharomyces cerevisiae.*
    c. *Bacillus subtilis.*
    d. live animals.
    e. live plants.

20. A cosmid is formed by combining a plasmid and a phage.
    a. True
    b. False

11   Physical and Chemical Control of Microbes

OVERVIEW

Control of microbial growth can be accomplished by physical methods, chemical methods, or a combination of the two. The choice of method should take into account the desired level of control—reduce numbers of all organisms, reduce numbers of a specific organism, or remove an organism associated with the object being treated. Consideration of the composition of the object to be treated must be made in selecting a method. Whichever method is used, exclusion of microbes will prevent the spread of infectious agents, slow down spoilage, and make products safe.

I.   INTRODUCTION

Concept: A variety of methods is used to exclude microbes from the environment.

II.   CONTROLLING MICROORGANISMS

Concept: Though possessing a long and eventful history, control of exposure to potentially harmful microbes is a great concern.

Objective 1.   Define sterilization, disinfection, antisepsis, bacteriostasis, sanitization, and degermation.

Objective 2.   Contrast germicide, disinfectant, antiseptic, bactericide, fungicide, virucide, sporocide, and biocide.

Objective 3.   Characterize microbial death.

Objective 4.   Enumerate factors that influence the action of antimicrobial agents.

Objective 5.   Discuss the modes of action of antimicrobial agents.

A.–B.   Fill in the puzzle on the following page.

The goal of sterilization procedures is the killing of which form of microbial life? What materials or substances typically require sterilization?

Why is sterilization *not* always considered practicable or necessary?

Give one example in which each procedure—disinfection, antisepsis, degerming, and sanitizing—is used.

A. Across

5. removes oils that lie on outer cutaneous layer and destroys pathogens that lie on skin surface
6. process that eliminates, through destruction or removal, all viable microorganisms, including viruses
9. cleaning technique that mechanically removes microorganisms to cut down on their numbers
10. procedure that destroys pathogenic and other harmful microbes, but not bacterial endospores
12. temporarily prevents microbes from multiplying, but does not kill outright
13. destroy or inhibit vegetative pathogens on exposed body surfaces

B. Down

1. chemical agent that kills pathogenic microorganisms
2. chemical agent that destroys pathogens on the body
3. chemical known to inactivate viruses, especially on living tissue
4. kills all living things, particularly microorganisms
5. chemical agent used to destroy pathogenic and other harmful microbes (not endospores) on inanimate objects
7. chemical sterilant destroys the most resistant of all microbes
8. aimed at destroying bacteria except those in the endospore stage
11. chemical that can destroy fungal spores, and hyphae, and yeasts

C. Define microbial death.

Can "microbial death" and "microbistasis" be used interchangeably? Why or why not?

D. List the factors, besides time, that influence the action of antimicrobial agents.

E. Briefly explain how antimicrobial agents work on the:

cell wall—

cell membrane—

protein and nucleic acid synthesis—

alteration of protein function—

74

III. METHODS OF PHYSICAL CONTROL

Concept: Though microorganisms have adapted to severe conditions of temperature, moisture, pressure, and light, the vast majority of microbes cannot survive sudden drastic changes in their environment.

Objective 1. Distinguish between and identify examples of methods of moist and dry heat.
Objective 2. Explain the importance of time and temperature as they affect microbial death by heat treatment.
Objective 3. Discuss four methods of heat control of microbial growth.
Objective 4. Describe the method of microbial control employed by cold, desiccation, radiation, sound waves, and filtration. Indicate the effectiveness of each method.

A. Matching.

    ___ flame   a. moist heat
    ___ hot water   b. dry heat
    ___ boiling water
    ___ electric heating coil
    ___ steam

What is the mode of action of:

moist heat—

dry heat—

B. Define thermal death time.

C. An autoclave is an example of microbial control by which method of moist heat?

How is sterilization achieved by an autoclave?

List two advantages and one disadvantage of autoclaving as a microbial control agent. What materials are most often sterilized by this method?

Describe the technique for intermittent sterilization.

Why would intermittent sterilization be used instead of autoclaving?

Boiling water is a form of disinfection, not sterilization. Why?

What is the greatest disadvantage of the boiling water method?

Pasteurization is a technique in which heat is applied to liquids in an effort to kill potential agents of infection and spoilage, while at the same time retaining flavor and food value. Relate the methods used for pasteurization.

D. Cold and desiccation (drying) tend to retard the growth of microbes instead of destroying the cells. These methods may be combined to preserve microbial cells in the process of freeze-drying called _____.

Define radiation (cold sterilization).

Distinguish between and give examples of ionizing and nonionizing radiation.

What materials are most often sterilized with ionizing radiation? Why is this the preferred method of sterilization?

Sonication (sound waves) is most effective against which type of microbe?

Discuss the theoretical basis for filter sterilizing air and liquids.

IV. CHEMICAL AGENTS IN MICROBIAL CONTROL

Concept: Antimicrobial chemicals include liquids, gases, and solids, with a range of use from disinfection to sterilization.

Objective 1. Identify the desirable qualities of a germicide, and distinguish between the three levels of chemical decontamination.

Objective 2. Identify the factors that affect the germicidal activity of chemicals.

Objective 3. Describe the forms, modes of action, specific applications, and limitations of: halogens, phenol, chlorhexidine, alcohols, hydrogen peroxide, detergents, heavy metals, aldehydes, gaseous sterilants, dyes, acids, and alkalies.

A. List the properties considered desirable of a germicide.

Contrast high, intermediate, and low levels of chemical decontamination, and include an example of use for each level of chemical.

B. List the factors affecting the germicidal activity of chemicals.

C. Complete the table.

Chemical	Forms	Modes of action	Specific applications	Limitations
halogens				
phenol				
chlorhexidine				
alcohols				
hydrogen peroxide				
detergents				
heavy metals				
aldehydes				
gaseous sterilants				
dyes				
acids				
alkalies				

V. SELF-TEST

1. Removal of contaminants (unwanted microorganisms) can be accomplished by
   a. physical agents.
   b. chemical agents.
   c. overlapping physical and chemical agents.
   d. all of the above.
   e. none of the above.

2. Which of the following have the highest resistance to physical and chemical control?
   a. bacterial vegetative cells
   b. bacterial endospores
   c. protozoan cysts
   d. fungal sexual spores
   e. enveloped viruses

3. Most infectious diseases of humans and animals are caused by non-spore-forming microbes.
   a. True
   b. False

4. All of the following are practical concerns in microbial control *except*
   a. Is sterilization required or is disinfection adequate?
   b. Is the item to be reused or permanently discarded?
   c. Will the agent emit an unpleasant odor?
   d. Will the agent penetrate the material to the extent that is necessary?
   e. Is the method cost and labor efficient, and is it safe?

5. Extremely high temperatures exceeding the maximum are _____, whereas temperatures below the minimum tend to have _____ effects.
   a. microbicidal, microbicidal
   b. microbistatic, microbistatic
   c. microbicidal, microbistatic
   d. microbistatic, microbicidal
   e. none of the above

6. At a given temperature, moist heat works several times faster than dry heat. For a constant length of exposure, moist heat kills cells at a higher temperature than dry heat.
   a. True
   b. False

7. With steam under pressure, it is not the pressure by itself that kills microbes, but the increased temperature that it produces.
   a. True
   b. False

8. An autoclave is an excellent device to sterilize
   a. glassware.
   b. cloth.
   c. metallic instruments.
   d. heat-resistant plastics.
   e. all of the above.

9. A germicide will be most effective in all of the following situations *except*
   a. materials contaminated with vegetative cells.
   b. adequate contact time for the chemical to penetrate the contaminated item.
   c. materials characterized as a smooth, solid object.
   d. materials possessing large amounts of organic matter.
   e. materials contaminated with a moderate microbial load.

10. Which chemical is the most effective in the sterilization of plastic materials and delicate instruments?
    a. alcohol
    b. ethylene oxide
    c. hydrogen peroxide
    d. heavy metals
    e. aldehydes

11. The elimination of all viable agents is called
    a. pasteurization.
    b. sterilization.
    c. desiccation.
    d. sanitization.
    e. disinfection.

12. Which of these chemicals can sterilize?
    a. alcohol
    b. phenol
    c. glutaraldehyde
    d. chlorine
    e. soap

13. Which of the following affects the elimination of bacteria from an object?
    a. number of bacteria present
    b. presence of organic matter
    c. concentration of the agent
    d. temperature and pH
    e. all of the above

14. Bacterial death will result from damage to which of the following structures?
    a. cell wall
    b. plasma (cell) membrane
    c. proteins
    d. nucleic acids
    e. all of the above

15. The higher the concentration of a chemical agent, the more germicidal it is.
    a. True
    b. False

Matching.

____ 16. germicide
____ 17. disinfection
____ 18. antisepsis
____ 19. bacteriostatic
____ 20. sanitation

a. reduce agents on body surface
b. inhibits growth
c. pathogens killed on an inanimate surface
d. dish cleaning technique
e. general killing term

12 Drugs, Microbes, Host—The Elements of Chemotherapy

OVERVIEW

The search for an antimicrobial "magic bullet" continues. The unique characteristics of each type of microorganism, combined with the condition and characteristics of the host, complicate the process of finding the chemotherapeutic agent that kills the microbe without harming the host. Meanwhile, currently available antimicrobials (antibiotics, antifungals, antiparasitic, and antihelminthic drugs) are used to control or prevent disease with possible adverse reactions in the host.

I. INTRODUCTION

Concept: Chemotherapy is the use of chemicals to control or prevent infection.

II. PRINCIPLES OF ANTIMICROBIAL THERAPY

Concept: Historically, humans have been taking medicines for diseases (chemotherapy) for thousands of years.

Objective 1. Discuss the current term *antimicrobic* as it relates to antibiotics and synthetics.
Objective 2. Recognize the aim of anti-infective therapy.
Objective 3. Identify the origins of antimicrobial drugs.

A. Exemplify the traditional separation of antimicrobial drugs into two categories.

Define:

antibiotics—

synthetics—

B. State the aim of anti-infective therapy.

Explain the concept of selective toxicity as it applies to the use of antimicrobial drugs.

C. The greatest number of antibiotics is derived from which genera of:

bacteria—

molds—

III. CHARACTERISTIC INTERACTIONS BETWEEN DRUG AND MICROBE

Concept: Selective toxicity is best demonstrated by drugs that block the actions or synthesis of molecules found in microorganisms but not in vertebrate cells.

Objective 1. Identify and discuss in detail four mechanisms of drug action.
Objective 2. Describe the acquisition and development of drug resistance.

A. Explain the four mechanisms of drug action and give an example of each.

inhibit cell wall synthesis—

inhibit nucleic acid synthesis—

inhibit protein synthesis—

interfere with the function of the cell membrane—

B. Summarize each of the two major genetic events that create drug resistance:

spontaneous chromosomal mutation—

transfer of extrachromosomal DNA from a resistant species to a sensitive species (plasmid)—

Name three methods bacteria use to transfer resistance factors (R factors) among themselves.

List the specific mechanisms of drug resistance.

Explain natural selection.

Name three strategies for limiting development of drug-resistant strains of microorganisms.

IV. SURVEY OF MAJOR ANTIMICROBIAL DRUG GROUPS

Concept: There are many different antimicrobials, each known by many different names and belonging to 20 drug families.

Objective 1. Characterize the different natural antibacterial drugs.
Objective 2. Characterize the different synthetic antimicrobial drugs.
Objective 3. Characterize the different drugs used to treat fungal infections.
Objective 4. Characterize the different drugs used to treat parasitic infections.
Objective 5. Characterize the different drugs used to treat viral infections.

A. Fill in the puzzle.

Across

2. component of ointment used in combatting superficial skin infections
4. broad spectrum, high toxicity to bone marrow
6. use limited by toxicity to the kidneys
7. used in treating penicillin- and methicillin-resistant staphylococcal infections
8. figures prominently in treating mycobacterial infections
10. exclusive products of *Streptomyces* and *Micromonospora*
11. Imipenem; broad spectrum, active in small concentrations, low human toxicity

Down

1. drug of choice for *Mycoplasma, Legionella,* and *Chlamydia*
3. ampicillin, amoxicillin
4. root "-cef" is part of antibiotic name
5. broadest spectrum, low toxicity
9. limited application due to tendency to cause adverse reactions in the gastrointestinal tract

List two new classes of antibiotics and describe their use.

B. Discuss the use of the following synthetics:

sulfonamides—

sulfones—

trimethoprim—

Name three antimicrobials used against *M. tuberculosis.*

C. Treatment of fungal infections presents special problems. Indicate the causes of these problems.

Describe the use of these drugs in treating fungal infections:

amphotericin B—

nystatin—

griseofulvin—

azoles—

flucytosine—

D. Fill in the blank.

Antiparasitic drug	Effective in treating infections caused by:
quinine	_____
Flagyl	_____
Thiabendazole	_____
piperazine	_____
niclosamide	_____
praziquantel	_____

E. The major limitations of antiviral agents include:

Describe the action and indicate the use of:

acyclovir—

ribavirin—

azidothymidine—

saquinavir and ritonivir—

amantadine—

interferon—

List some currently approved anti-AIDS drugs.

V. CHARACTERISTICS OF HOST-DRUG REACTIONS

Concept: Careful consideration of host/drug reactions is required in the selection of an antimicrobial drug.

Objective 1. Discuss in some detail the major side effects of drugs.
Objective 2. Detail the information necessary to make a responsible drug choice for antimicrobial treatment.

A. List the major organs affected by drug toxicity.

Explain the stimulation of an allergic response by a drug.

Define normal flora.

Define superinfection.

Provide an example of a situation in which chemotherapy may cause a disturbance of the normal flora.

B. Explain the importance of identifying the infectious agent before selecting an antimicrobial drug for treatment.

Outline the steps involved in the Kirby-Bauer technique used to test drug susceptibility of a microorganism.

Explain the significance of establishing the minimum inhibitory concentration (MIC) of an antimicrobic.

Define therapeutic index as related to host toxicity.

Review the importance of a patient's medical history, including how any preexisting medical conditions and/or current intake of other drugs would affect the physician's decision concerning the drug of choice in treatment with an antimicrobic.

List the problems associated with the use of antimicrobial drugs without the proper education on their appropriate usage.

VI. SELF-TEST

1. Antimicrobial agents effective against a wide range of different microbes are considered
    a. narrow spectrum.
    b. broad spectrum.
    c. undesirable.
    d. unavailable.
    e. none of these.

2. Penicillins are less toxic to humans because they
    a. inhibit cell wall synthesis.
    b. inhibit nucleic acid synthesis.
    c. inhibit protein synthesis.
    d. interfere with the function of the cell membrane.
    e. all of the above.

3. Antibiotics that affect cell wall synthesis are considered bactericidal because
    a. the cells will shrink when exposed to a hypotonic environment.
    b. the cells will shrink when exposed to a hypertonic environment.
    c. the cells will lyse when exposed to a hypotonic environment.
    d. the cells will lyse when exposed to a hypertonic environment.
    e. none of the above.

4. Microbial inactivation of drugs occurs almost exclusively through enzymes that permanently alter drug structure.
    a. True
    b. False

5. Synthetic antimicrobics as a group originate from bacterial or fungal fermentations.
    a. True
    b. False

6. Isoniazid is used to treat
   a. staph infections.
   b. pneumonia.
   c. meningitis.
   d. tuberculosis.
   e. skin infections.

7. Helminths are larger parasites that are closer to humans in cellular physiology. The most effective antihelminthics
   a. block reproduction of the worm.
   b. interfere with cell wall synthesis of the worm.
   c. immobilize, disintegrate, or block the metabolism of the worm.
   d. none of the above.
   e. all of the above.

8. Major conclusions regarding interferon therapy include that it
   a. does not cure viral infections; it mainly reduces healing time and complications.
   b. may prevent some symptoms of cold and papilloma viruses.
   c. is somewhat toxic if given in large doses.
   d. apparently slows the progress of a few cancers (bone, breast).
   e. all of the above.

9. Major side effects of drugs fall into each of the following categories *except*
   a. direct damage to tissue through toxicity.
   b. allergic reactions.
   c. disruption in the balance of normal microbial flora.
   d. destruction of the harmful organism.
   e. none of the above.

10. A physician often chooses to begin initial antimicrobial therapy based on the principle of "informed" best guess.
    a. True
    b. False

11. Drug resistance means that
    a. the host's immune system prevents the drug from working.
    b. the drug cannot protect a particular organism.
    c. the drug cannot damage a particular organism.
    d. a particular organism is susceptible to damage by the drug.
    e. all of the above.

12. Most of the available antimicrobials are effective against
    a. viruses.
    b. bacteria.
    c. fungi.
    d. protozoans.
    e. all of the above.

13. Which of the following antimicrobials is recommended for use against fungal infections?
    a. polymixin
    b. bacitracin
    c. cephalosporin
    d. amphotericin
    e. penicillin

14. Protozoan and helminthic diseases are hard to treat because
    a. they don't reproduce.
    b. they don't have ribosomes.
    c. they reproduce inside host cells.
    d. their cells are structurally and functionally similar to human cells.
    e. none of the above.

15. Neosporin contains neomycin, polymixin, and
    a. penicillin.
    b. bacitracin.
    c. cephalosporin.
    d. rifampin.
    e. vancomycin.

16. Tetracyclines are considered broad-spectrum antibiotics.
    a. True
    b. False

17. Semisynthetics are chemically altered
    antibiotics.
    a. True
    b. False

18. Penicillin is somewhat more toxic to human
    cells than is amphotericin.
    a. True
    b. False

19. An antimicrobic drug must be more toxic to
    the host than to the pathogen.
    a. True
    b. False

20. The reason for producing semisynthetic
    antibiotics is to convert naturally occurring
    antibiotics into forms that produce the
    development of resistant strains.
    a. True
    b. False

13 Microbe–Human Interactions: Infection and Disease

OVERVIEW

Constant exposure to microbes inevitably leads to infection provided the size of inoculum and portal of entry into the body are such that infection results. Microbial invasion and establishment in the host tissues bring on the development of signs and symptoms of disease. As microorganisms exit the body, they may be transmitted to other individuals if the disease is communicable.

I. INTRODUCTION

Concept: Microbes and humans can coexist in balance without disease, an imbalance may result in disease.

II. THE HUMAN HOST

Concept: The nature of the human-microorganism interrelationship, whether mutual, commensal, or parasitic, is that it begins with contact.

> **Objective 1.** Discuss the development of normal resident flora in the human body.
> **Objective 2.** Indicate the significance of normal indigenous flora in specific regions of the human body.

A. Describe the touchdown, colonization, and localization of the normal resident flora in the human body.

Although relatively stable, list the causes of flora fluctuation.

Explain the medical importance of a shift in the balance of the flora.

Outline the initial colonization of the newborn.

B. Summarize (include effect of human anatomy on the flora, location of the flora, and organisms involved) the information for each specific body region.

skin—

alimentary tract—

mouth—

large intestine—

respiratory tract—

genitourinary tract—

What is meant by "germ-free" animals?

Explain the results of experiments with germ-free animals.

III. THE PROGRESS OF AN INFECTION

Concept: Pathogenic organisms enter the body, attach, invade, and multiply in target tissue and are finally released.

Objective 1. Distinguish between pathogenicity and virulence.
Objective 2. List the various portals of entry and indicate some examples of the microorganisms that would choose each particular mode of entry.

A. Define:

true pathogen—

opportunistic pathogen—

List some factors that predispose a person to opportunistic infections.

Explain the key difference between pathogenicity and virulence.

B. Match the organism with its possible portal of entry (entries).

___ *Pneumocystis*	a. skin
___ *Toxoplasma gondii* (toxoplasmosis)	b. gastrointestinal
___ *Candida albicans*	c. respiratory tract
___ *Giardia lamblia*	d. urogenital tract
___ *Escherichia coli*	e. placenta
___ *Staphylococcus aureus*	
___ *Trichomonas*	
___ *Mycobacterium tuberculosis*	
___ *Treponema pallidum* (syphilis)	
___ *Streptococcus pyogenes*	

IV. MECHANISMS OF INVASION AND ESTABLISHMENT OF THE PATHOGEN

Concept: After gaining entry into the host, the pathogen must bind to the host, penetrate the epithelial boundary, and become established in the tissues to produce infection.

Objective 1. Correlate pathogenic adhesion and the specificity of the pathogen.
Objective 2. Describe the properties of a pathogen that endow it with the ability to penetrate the epithelial boundary of the host.
Objective 3. Discuss the establishment of the pathogen in the host tissues and the pathologic effects produced by the pathogen.
Objective 4. List the various portals of exit and indicate the microorganisms that would choose each particular mode of exit.
Objective 5. Illustrate how a microbe may remain in the body, producing a latent infection.

A. Define adhesion.

The specific interaction of microbial attachment to the host cell involves
_____ on the microbial surface reacting with
_____ on the host cell.

B. Explain the mechanism of each of the following virulence factors:

enzymes—

exotoxins—

endotoxins—

antiphagocytic factors—

C. Besides the adverse effects caused by the factors mentioned above, list the additional damage
    inflicted by the microbes on the target organ.

Matching.

____ microbe found in several sites and tissue fluids	a. localized
____ infectious agents break loose from a local infection and	b. systemic
seed the body	c. focal
____ infection that remains confined to a specific body site	d. mixed
____ rapid onset, severe, and short-lived effects	e. primary
____ first infection contracted, though multiple infections are	f. secondary
occurring in the same episode	g. acute
____ intermediate infection, onset not as rapid nor as persistent	h. chronic
____ synergistic, the microbes cooperate	i. subacute
____ progress and persist over a long period	
____ second infection caused by a different microbe, though	
multiple infections are occurring in the same episode	

Distinguish between a sign and a symptom.

List the symptoms of inflammation.

List the signs of inflammation.

Leukocytosis and leukopenia are blood signs of infection; differentiate between the two.

Define septicemia.

D. Match the portal of exit with the appropriate disease or agent of disease.

___ warts
___ AIDS virus
___ fecal contaminants
___ measles
___ *Chlamydia*
___ influenza
___ *Candida albicans*
___ mononucleosis virus
___ hepatitis virus

a. respiratory tract
b. saliva
c. skin
d. gastrointestinal tract
e. urogenital tract
f. blood

E. Relate an example of a latent infection.

V. EPIDEMIOLOGY: THE STUDY OF DISEASE IN POPULATIONS

Concept: Epidemiology is the science that examines every aspect of the determinants and distribution of any disease, infectious or otherwise.

Objective 1. Discuss the who, when, where, how, what, and why of disease.

A. Physicians and hospitals report all notifiable diseases that are brought to their attention to the
_____ _____ _____ _____ . They in turn
report to the _____ _____ _____ in Atlanta, Georgia, which
publishes the weekly *Mortality and Morbidity Report.* Ultimately, the CDC shares its statistics on
disease with the _____ _____ _____ for worldwide
tabulation and control.

Distinguish between prevalence and incidence.

Differentiate:

endemic—

sporadic—

epidemic—

pandemic—

Distinguish between reservoir and source.

What type of reservoir includes persons and animals?

Nonliving reservoirs include _____ and _____ .

Define carrier.

Asymptomatic (showing no symptoms) carriers can be _____ carriers or
_____ carriers depending upon the stage of infection.

Contrast active and passive carriers.

Define vector.

Differentiate biological vectors from mechanical vectors.

Define and give an example of zoonosis.

Distinguish between communicable and non-communicable infectious diseases.

Transmission patterns in communicable diseases can be divided into two major categories:
_____ _____ and _____ _____ .

Relate an example of transmission as accomplished by:

direct transfer—

common vehicle transfer—

fomite transfer—

airborne transfer—

Where are nosocomial infections acquired?

96

Factors accounting for the prevalence of nosocomial infections include the availability of a reservoir, a compromised host, and a mode of transmission. Account for the availability of these factors.

Distinguish between isolation and reverse isolation.

List Koch's postulates as established to determine the precise etiology (cause) of the disease.

VI. SELF-TEST

1. The pattern of the host-parasite relationship is an unalterable continuum beginning with contamination, progressing to infection, and ending in disease.
   a. True
   b. False

2. Following establishment, the normal resident flora modifies its microhabitat by
   a. altering the pH and oxygen tension.
   b. excreting chemicals such as fatty acids, gases, alcohol, and antibiotics.
   c. creating physical obstacles.
   d. all of the above.
   e. none of the above.

3. An example of how one would contract transient flora of the skin is
   a. during the birthing process.
   b. through breast-feeding.
   c. by making mudpies as a child.
   d. by contact with family members.
   e. through the first foods taken in as an infant.

4. If the size of the inoculum is smaller than the infectious dose,
   a. infection will generally not progress.
   b. infection will generally progress at a very slow rate.
   c. infection will generally progress at a moderate rate.
   d. infection will generally progress at a rapid rate.
   e. infection will generally progress at a very rapid rate.

5. Exogenous infectious agents originate from
   a. the environment.
   b. a latent infection.
   c. another person.
   d. a and b.
   e. a and c.

6. What is necrosis?
   a. growth of tissue
   b. death of tissue
   c. division of tissue cells
   d. increased cellular metabolism
   e. none of the above

7. Toxins travel through the blood from the area of microbial multiplication to the target tissue, causing a _____ infection.
   a. localized
   b. systemic
   c. focal
   d. toxemic
   e. chronic

8. An active infection that produces no noticeable symptoms is termed
   a. subclinical.
   b. inapparent.
   c. silent.
   d. asymptomatic.
   e. all of the above.

9. All cases of infection in the community are diagnosed and reported so the CDC figures correspond to the actual occurrence of disease.
   a. True
   b. False

10. When the agent is highly transmissible, especially through direct contact, the disease is
    a. communicable.
    b. non-communicable.
    c. contagious.
    d. asymptomatic.
    e. non-invasive.

11. Normally, microbes are found in all of these except the
    a. vagina.
    b. alimentary tract.
    c. conjunctiva.
    d. blood.
    e. urine.

12. A sexually transmitted disease is an example of what mode of transmission?
    a. droplet
    b. fomite
    c. vector
    d. airborne
    e. direct contact

13. A needle stick is an example of what mode of transmission?
    a. droplet
    b. fomite
    c. vector
    d. airborne
    e. direct contact

14. The largest variety of microbes is found in/on the
    a. mouth.
    b. skin.
    c. genitals.
    d. trachea.
    e. colon.

15. Plague transmitted by a flea is an example of what mode of transmission?
    a. droplet
    b. fomite
    c. vector
    d. airborne
    e. direct contact

16. Opportunistic infections require
    a. a healthy host.
    b. a vector.
    c. a compromised host.
    d. oxygen be present.
    e. none of the above.

17. If a common cold creates conditions that allow *Streptococcus* to invade the middle ear, the *Streptococcus* infection is called
    a. an opportunistic infection.
    b. a secondary infection.
    c. a primary infection.
    d. a mixed infection.
    e. an acute infection.

18. An infection that occurs in many nations is
    a. endemic.
    b. sporadic.
    c. epidemic.
    d. pandemic.
    e. prevalent.

19. A person who has a pathogen but never manifests signs is a/an
    a. reservoir.
    b. active carrier.
    c. passive carrier.
    d. asymptomatic carrier.
    e. convalescent carrier.

20. An infection such as tetanus from stepping on a dirty nail is
    a. communicable.
    b. non-communicable.
    c. contagious.
    d. spread by direct contact.
    e. vector transmitted.

14   The Nature of Host Defenses

OVERVIEW

The human body's defenses are varied and interwoven. The natural, inborn, nonspecific defenses include physical, chemical, and genetic barriers. Immune reactions happen at the molecular level and include phagocytosis and inflammation. Specific immunity results from a dual system of B and T lymphocytes. The cooperation of these defenses normally provides protection against infection and disease.

I.   INTRODUCTION

Concept: Human defenses, nonspecific and specific, resist infection and disease caused by harmful microbes.

II. DEFENSE MECHANISMS OF THE HOST IN PERSPECTIVE

Concept: Protection from microbial infection includes the first, second, and third lines of host defense functioning as an integrated whole.

Objective 1.   Discuss the nonspecific first line of host defense against infection.
Objective 2.   Identify the second and third lines of host defense against infection.

A.   Physical or anatomical barriers of the skin and mucous membranes prevent the entry of infectious organisms. Explain the methodology of the various barrier mechanisms:

compacted intact epithelium—

sweat, mucous, tears, saliva, urine—

hairs in nose—

ciliated epithelium—

normal flora—

Nonspecific chemical defenses involve enzymes (lysozyme in tears and saliva), pH (skin—fatty acid; stomach—hydrochloric acid), and normal flora. True/False

"Humans can't acquire distemper from cats, and cats can't get mumps from humans." Why?

B.   What are the second and third lines of host defense against infection?

III.   INTRODUCING THE IMMUNE SYSTEM

Concept: The immune system functions at the molecular level.

   Objective 1.   Relate markers, surveillance, and recognition to the immune response.

A.   Define marker.

Describe the process that detects markers—surveillance.

Explain the recognition of markers.

IV.   SYSTEMS INVOLVED IN IMMUNE DEFENSES

Concept: The immune system is not a single, well-defined site but a merging of four main body compartments: the reticuloendothelial system, the extracellular spaces around tissue cells, the bloodstream, and the lymphatic system.

   Objective 1.   Explain the significance of the reticuloendothelial system to the immune response.
   Objective 2.   Discuss the composition and function of the blood components of the circulatory system.
   Objective 3.   Summarize the composition and function of the lymphatic system.

A.   The reticuloendothelial system is intrinsic to the immune response because it:

B.   Distinguish between plasma and serum.

Define hemopoiesis.

The ultimate precursors of new blood cells are the _____ _____. These cells will eventually differentiate into the red blood cells, white blood cells, and platelets.

Matching.

____ largest white blood cell	a. neutrophils (55% to 90% of circulating WBCs)
____ high levels observed in parasitic infections	b. eosinophils (1% to 3% of circulating WBCs)
____ band (horseshoe-shaped nucleus) or seg (multilobed nucleus)	c. basophils (.5% of circulating WBCs)
____ function primarily in hemostasis	d. monocytes (3% to 7% of circulating WBCs)
____ main work is phagocytosis	
____ prominent dark blue to black granules	e. lymphocytes (20% to 35% of circulating WBCs)
____ bilobed nucleus, red granules	
____ leave circulation and differentiate into macrophages	f. erythrocyte (RBC)
____ act primarily in immediate allergy and inflammation	g. platelet
____ exist as B and T cells	
____ transport gases to and from cells	

The movement of white blood cells from the blood into the tissue spaces is _____.

C. Contrast diapedesis and chemotaxis. List the three major functions of the lymphatic system.

The liquid found within the lymphatic system is called _____. The composition of this fluid parallels that of _____.

The lymphatic capillaries feed into fewer and larger vessels that, in turn, drain into two ducts, the contents of which flow in one direction—_____ _____ _____.

Fill in the chart.

Lymphatic organ/tissue	Description	Location	Function
lymph nodes			
spleen			
thymus			
tonsils			
GALT			

V. NONSPECIFIC IMMUNE REACTIONS OF THE BODY'S COMPARTMENTS

Concept: Generalized mechanisms that are part of the host defenses include: inflammation, phagocytosis, interferon, and complement.

      Objective 1.   Describe in detail the inflammatory response, including its adjunct component—fever.
      Objective 2.   Indicate which cells are involved in phagocytosis and discuss their activities with respect to the immune response.
      Objective 3.   Illustrate the immunological role of complement and interferon.

A.   List the chief functions of inflammation.

Summarize the events producing inflammation following tissue injury:

vascular changes—

edema and chemotaxis—

repair—

Define fever.

A pyrogen produces fever by resetting the thermostat in the _____.

List the benefits of fever.

B.   List the general activities of phagocytes.

Name the three main types of phagocytes.

Discuss the entire scope of overlapping but separable events of phagocytosis including:

chemotaxis—

ingestion—

phagolysosome formation—

destruction—

elimination—

C. Describe the action of the antiviral interferon.

What three kinds of cells produce interferon?

Summarize the three stages making up the complement cascade.

VI. SPECIFIC IMMUNITIES—THE THIRD AND FINAL LINE OF DEFENSE

Concept: When host barriers and nonspecific defenses fail to contain an infectious agent, specific immunity comes to the rescue.

VII. SELF-TEST

1. By what mechanism(s) does lacrimation (tearing) provide defense from microbial infection?
    a. provides a physical barrier
    b. flushes away irritants
    c. contains lysozyme
    d. a and b
    e. b and c

2. Genetic defenses include
    a. species specificity.
    b. a gene for sickle-cell anemia providing resistance to malaria.
    c. racial differences.
    d. ethnic differences.
    e. all of the above.

3. The immune system is programmed to recognize non-self (foreign markers) and to entrap and destroy foreign invaders.
    a. True
    b. False

4. Serum can clot and plasma cannot.
    a. True
    b. False

5. Morphologically and functionally similar to basophils, these cells are bound to connective tissue.
    a. neutrophils
    b. eosinophils
    c. mast cells
    d. monocytes
    e. lymphocytes

6. The producers of antibodies are plasma cells formed from
   a. B lymphocytes.
   b. eosinophils.
   c. monocytes.
   d. neutrophils.
   e. T lymphocytes.

7. The benefits of inflammatory edema and chemotaxis include
   a. the fluid influx that dilutes toxic substances.
   b. a fibrin mesh that traps and localizes microbes.
   c. aggregate neutrophils phagocytizing and destroying microbes.
   d. all of the above.
   e. none of the above.

8. The phagocytes that respond early in the inflammatory response to bacteria are the
   a. macrophages.
   b. eosinophils.
   c. neutrophils.
   d. lymphocytes.
   e. none of the above.

9. This membrane attack complex digests holes in the cell membranes of bacterial cells and enveloped viruses, thereby destroying them.
   a. interferon
   b. complement
   c. lymphokine
   d. cytokine
   e. none of the above

10. Acquired immunity is characterized by
    a. specificity.
    b. memory.
    c. longevity.
    d. a and b.
    e. a and c.

11. The human body is armed with various levels of defense, each acting in a completely separate fashion.
    a. True
    b. False

12. The process of searching the body for any markers that are new and different (nonself) is
    a. surveillance.
    b. recognition.
    c. recognizance.
    d. territoriality.
    e. none of the above.

13. Fever is beneficial because
    a. it inhibits multiplication of temperature sensitive microorganisms.
    b. it impedes bacterial nutrition by reducing the availability of iron.
    c. it increases metabolism in the person with the fever.
    d. it stimulates the immune response in the person with the fever.
    e. all of the above.

14. Chills are a sign that
    a. body temperature is falling.
    b. body temperature is rising.
    c. body temperature will remain the same.
    d. sweating will follow.
    e. none of the above.

15. In cell-mediated immunity, these cells help, suppress, and modulate immune functions and kill foreign cells.
    a. B lymphocytes
    b. eosinophils
    c. monocytes
    d. neutrophils
    e. T lymphocytes

16. Many of the initial encounters between lymphocytes and microbes that result in specific immune responses occur in the
    a. lymph nodes.
    b. spleen.
    c. liver.
    d. thymus.
    e. GALT (gut associated lymphoid tissue).

17. The thymus plays a major role in
    a. phagocytosis.
    b. inflammation.
    c. maturation of T lymphocytes.
    d. maturation of B lymphocytes.
    e. circulating blood for filtration.

18. Vasoconstriction following an injury causes
    an increased inflow of blood to the area,
    resulting in redness and localized warmth.
    a. True
    b. False

19. The overall stages in the complement
    cascade include all except
    a. initiation.
    b. amplification.
    c. cascade.
    d. membrane attack.
    e. termination.

20. Complement exhibits two schemes, the
    classical pathway and the alternative
    pathway. What is/are the difference(s) in
    the two?
    a. how they are activated
    b. the blood proteins (factors) involved
    c. speed and efficiency
    d. a and b
    e. a and c

15 The Acquisition of Specific Immunity and Its Applications

OVERVIEW

In the chapter before this one, the concept of immunity was introduced. In this chapter, the five stages involved in a specific immune response to an antigen are described in detail. The means by which humans acquire specific immunities can be categorized as active, passive, natural, and artificial.

I. INTRODUCTION

Concept: The immune system defends the body against microorganisms, cancer cells, and a wide variety of diseases.

II. FURTHER EXPLORATIONS INTO THE IMMUNE SYSTEM

Concept: Knowledge of some essential preliminary concepts is necessary for understanding the principle stages involved in the acquired immune response.

> **Objective 1.** Identify the five principal stages of immunologic development.
> **Objective 2.** Discuss thoroughly the formation, function, and significance of cell surface receptors.

A. List and briefly discuss the five stages in the development of dual immune responses.

B. List the major functions of receptors.

Compare major histocompatibility complex (MHC) with human leukocyte antigen (HLA).

Genes regulating and coding for the MHC of humans are located on the _____ chromosome.

Describe the functions of the three MHC groups that have been identified:

class I—

class II—

class III—

Explain the development of lymphocytes possessing different genetically programmed markers as described by the clonal selection theory.

Two important generalities of immune responsiveness one can derive from the clonal selection theory are:

How does one develop tolerance to self?

The receptor genes in B lymphocytes govern the synthesis of _____.

Describe the structure of an immunoglobulin (including the significance of the variable and constant regions).

III. THE LYMPHOCYTE RESPONSE SYSTEM IN DEPTH

Concept: Specific acquired immunity occurs in several sequential stages.

Objective 1. Compare and contrast the specific happenings in B-cell and T-cell maturation.
Objective 2. Relate the properties of antigens.
Objective 3. Describe the host response to antigens.
Objective 4. Review the clonal selection, expansion, and antibody production by B lymphocytes when exposed to an antigen.
Objective 5. Recall how T cells respond to an antigen.

A. Summarize how stem cells differentiate to form lymphocytes.

Indicate the site of maturation of:

B cells—

T cells—

B. Define antigen.

To be perceived as an antigen, a substance must meet certain requirements. List and discuss these requirements.

Define and give one example of a hapten.

Contrast autoantigens and alloantigens.

C. _____ and _____ are important in concentrating the antigens and circulating them thoroughly through all areas populated by lymphocytes so that they come in contact with the proper clone.

Macrophages are antigen-processing cells that present the antigen to the lymphocytes. The macrophage produces _____ to activate the _____. These cells, in turn, produce _____ that stimulates a general activity of committed B and T cells.

D. Characterize a blast.

Successive mitotic divisions of a blast increase the lymphocyte clone size. Contrast the plasma and memory cells formed.

The principle activity of an antibody is to unite with, immobilize, call attention to, or neutralize the antigen for which it was formed. True/False

Define opsonization.

Describe the results of an antibody reacting with complement.

Define neutralization.

Match the class of antibody to its biological function.

____ associated with allergy, worm infections	a. IgG
____ memory antibodies, long-term immunity	b. IgA
____ receptor on B cells	c. IgM
____ associated with mucous membranes	d. IgD
____ produced at first response to antigen	e. IgE

Antibodies are found in the _____ _____ fraction of serum.

A quantitative way of expressing the level or concentration of antibodies in serum is the

_____.

Overview (Humoral Immunity)

Primary Response The body's first exposure to an antigen begins with a latent period. The antigen is concentrated and is presented to clones of B cells. Plasma cells produce IgM. The shift to IgG increases the titer to a certain plateau, then tapers off to a low maintenance level.
Secondary Response (anamnestic response) When the body is exposed to the same antigen a second or subsequent time, the immune response is amplified. Memory B cells rapidly turn out antibodies to increase the titer to prevent the development of disease as a result of exposure to the antigen.

Explain the development and significance of monoclonal antibodies.

E. Simultaneously occurring with B-cell activity are the T-cell responses of cell-mediated immunity. T-cell lymphoblasts divide into _____ and _____ cells.

Matching.

____ graft rejection, recognize the target cell expressing a foreign antigen	a. T-helper cells
____ cytotoxity not restricted to a single type of antigen	b. T-suppressor cells
____ present the antigen, produce lymphokines	c. cytotoxic T cells
____ delayed response to allergen	d. natural killer cells
____ restrict rampant uncontrolled immune responses	e. delayed hyper-sensitivity T cells

IV. A PRACTICAL SCHEME FOR CLASSIFYING SPECIFIC IMMUNITIES

Concept: Four interrelated categories (active, passive, natural, artificial) describe the ways humans acquire immunities.

> **Objective 1.** Distinguish between active or passive immunity, and naturally or artificially acquired immunity.

A. Matching.
___ fetus receives tetanus antibodies
___ vaccination against polio
___ recovery from the mumps
___ injection of hepatitis B immune serum globulin
___ nursing infant receives antibodies
___ vaccination against pertussis
___ recovery from the measles
___ injection of rabies immune serum globulin

a. naturally acquired active immunity
b. naturally acquired passive immunity
c. artificially acquired active immunity
d. artificially acquired passive immunity

V. SELF-TEST

1. Related persons are likely to express identical MHC receptors.
   a. True
   b. False

2. With all lymphocyte-antigen interactions there must be a receptor in the immune repertoire uniquely specific for each different antigen.
   a. True
   b. False

3. Small foreign molecules consisting only of a determinant group and that are too small by themselves to elicit an immune response are termed
   a. antigens.
   b. carriers.
   c. haptens.
   d. antibodies.
   e. none of the above.

4. These cells engulf the antigen and alter it by partial degradation or addition of molecules, presumably to increase immunogenicity and recognition.
   a. T cells
   b. B cells
   c. lymphocytes
   d. macrophages
   e. none of the above

5. All antigens require the cooperation of macrophages or T-helper cells to trigger a general B-lymphocyte response.
   a. True
   b. False

6. The specificity of antigen binding sites for antigens is very similar to enzyme and substrate specificity.
   a. True
   b. False

7. Special types of antibodies that neutralize bacterial endotoxins are
   a. antigens.
   b. autoantigens.
   c. antitoxins.
   d. alloantigens.
   e. toxoids.

8. Which class of antibodies crosses the placenta to give passive immunity to the neonate.
   a. IgM
   b. IgD
   c. IgA
   d. IgE
   e. IgG

9. The concentration of antibodies expressed quantitatively is the
   a. volume.
   b. number.
   c. mass ratio.
   d. titer.
   e. none of the above.

10. Memory cells are
    a. B cells only.
    b. T cells only.
    c. B cells and T cells.
    d. macrophages.
    e. B cells, T cells, and macrophages.

11. Major functions of receptors include all except
    a. to perceive and attach to nonself or foreign molecules.
    b. to promote the recognition of self molecules.
    c. to receive and transmit chemical messages among other cells of the system.
    d. to make the cell membrane surface uneven.
    e. to aid in cellular development.

12. Put the stages involved in developing acquired specific immunity in order.
    1. Lymphocytes proliferate producing clones.
    2. Macrophages detect invading foreign antigens and present them to the lymphocytes.
    3. Activated T lymphocytes differentiate into one of four subtypes.
    4. Lymphocytes originate in hemopoietic tissue then diverge into two distinct types (B cells and T cells).
    5. Activated B lymphocytes become plasma cells that produce and secrete antibodies.

    a. 1, 2, 3, 4, 5
    b. 4, 2, 1, 5, 3
    c. 2, 5, 4, 1, 3
    d. 3, 1, 2, 5, 4
    e. 5, 2, 3, 1, 4

13. Lymphocyte differentiation and immunocompetence are basically complete by the
    a. late fetal period.
    b. late neonatal period.
    c. late infancy period.
    d. late childhood.
    e. adulthood.

14. Most materials that serve as antigens fall into the chemical category including
    a. proteins and polypeptides.
    b. lipoproteins.
    c. glycoproteins and nucleoproteins.
    d. polysaccharides and lipopolysaccharides.
    e. all of the above.

15. Autoantigens seem to account for some types of autoimmune diseases.
    a. True
    b. False

16. Antigens that evoke allergic responses are
    a. autoantigens.
    b. alloantigens.
    c. allergens.
    d. haptens.
    e. none of the above.

17. Which class of antibodies binds to basophils and mast cells causing the release of allergic mediators such as histamine?
    a. IgM
    b. IgD
    c. IgA
    d. IgE
    e. IgG

18. What is the basis for giving boosters, additional doses of vaccines?
    a. to produce antibodies to the first exposure to antigen
    b. to concentrate the antigen
    c. to initiate a primary immune response
    d. to increase serum titer
    e. none of the above

19. The most important cells contributing to graft rejection are
    a. B cells.
    b. T cells.
    c. macrophages.
    d. neutrophils.
    e. monocytes.

20. Passive immunity provides long-term protection from a particular disease
    a. True
    b. False

16 Immunization and Immune Assays

OVERVIEW

Biomedical applications of the immune system's response to antigens provide protection against disease and diagnosis of disease. Injection of immune globulin gives passive immunity to disease, protection that lasts 2–3 months, whereas injection of a vaccine gives active immunity to disease that confers long-lasting protection. Diagnosis of a disease or screening a population for a disease is accomplished by serological testing for antibodies to the causative antigen.

I. INTRODUCTION

Concept: Expanded knowledge of immune function has practical benefits in the development of vaccines and the testing of blood for signs of infection and disease.

II. PRACTICAL APPLICATIONS OF IMMUNOLOGIC FUNCTION

Concept: Protection against disease and diagnosis of disease are biomedical applications of knowledge about the immune system reactions.

Objective 1. Discuss the use of passive immunization to prevent the infection of exposed individuals.

Objective 2. Consider the preparation and use of vaccination for active artificial immunity.

Objective 3. Discuss the various serological and immune tests used to measure the immune response *in vitro* and *in vivo*.

A. Contrast immune serum globulin (ISG) and specific immune globulin (SIG).

Alternatives to the preferred human immune globulin are antisera and antitoxins produced in a suitable animal. Why aren't the animal sera, with a greater availability, the treatment of choice?

B. List the characteristics of a safe, effective vaccine.

Describe the preparation of these vaccines and give an example of each type:

killed, whole vaccine—

live, attenuated vaccine—

subunit, acellular vaccine—

Trojan horse vaccine—

anti-idiotype vaccine—

Relate the necessity of an adjuvant included in a vaccine.

In considering vaccination for the individual(s), the underlying philosophy is "risk vs. benefit." Enumerate some of the risks of vaccination.

Discuss benefits of vaccination in relationship to establishing herd immunity and disease eradication.

C. Explain the basis of serological testing.

Matching (*in vitro* testing).

____ serum proteins separated
____ sheep RBCs indicator, lysin-mediated hemolysis, rheumatic fever
____ used in blood banking/VDRL, antigen is whole cell
____ locate antigens in tissues, chlamydiosis
____ used in agar gel, antigen is a cell-free molecule in solution
____ used for positive HIV in the ELISA
____ uses horseradish peroxidase, which releases a dye when exposed to substrate, screen for HIV antibodies

a. agglutination reaction
b. precipitation reaction
c. immunoelectrophoresis
d. Western blot
e. complement fixation
f. immunofluorescence
g. ELISA

In vivo tests for antibodies are performed on the body itself. Provide an example of *in vivo* testing.

III. SELF-TEST

1. Most passive immunization involves the administration of antibodies, but occasionally these cells are given passively.
   a. macrophages
   b. B cells
   c. T cells
   d. plasma cells
   e. none of the above

2. A special type of acellular vaccine consisting of a purified exotoxin that has been chemically denatured is the
   a. adjuvant.
   b. Trojan horse.
   c. killed, whole.
   d. antitoxin.
   e. toxoid.

3. Routes of administration of vaccines include all *except*
   a. oral.
   b. intradermal.
   c. intramuscular.
   d. intravenous.
   e. subcutaneous.

4. Serological testing has expanded to include
   a. urine.
   b. cerebrospinal fluid.
   c. saliva.
   d. whole tissues.
   e. all of the above.

5. Serological tests are specific (focus on a certain antibody or antigen) and sensitive (detect even very small amounts of antibodies or antigens).
   a. True
   b. False

6. A positive reaction in a serological test indicates that the patient has the disease.
   a. True
   b. False

7. When serological testing is done to diagnose current disease,
   a. one test showing seropositive is sufficient.
   b. symptoms and one seropositive test are sufficient.
   c. a series of tests to show a rising antibody titer is necessary.
   d. a series of tests to show a decreasing antibody titer is necessary.
   e. none of the above.

8. The antigen-antibody reaction occurs on the molecular level and is clearly visible to the naked eye; no indicator is necessary.
   a. True
   b. False

9. In the double diffusion method or agar gel precipitation,
   a. both antigens and antibodies diffuse.
   b. placing antigen in the center well can assess the content of sera in the outer wells.
   c. placing antiserum in the center well can help identify antigens placed in the outer wells.
   d. all of the above.
   e. none of the above.

10. The test that measures IgE in allergic patients is the
    a. agglutination reaction.
    b. precipitation reaction.
    c. complement fixation test.
    d. immunofluorescence test.
    e. radioimmunosorbent test.

11. A vaccine must be considered from which of the following standpoints?
    a. antigen selection
    b. effectiveness
    c. ease in administration
    d. safety and cost
    e. all of the above

12. Antigenic stimulants in vaccine preparations include all of the following except
    a. killed whole cells or inactivated viruses.
    b. live, attenuated cells or viruses.
    c. immune serum globulin.
    d. parts of cells or viruses (subunits).
    e. genetically engineered microbes or microbial parts.

13. Advantages to live vaccine preparations include all except
    a. viable organisms can multiply and produce infection (but not disease) like a natural organism.
    b. they confer long-lasting protection.
    c. they usually require fewer doses than other types of vaccine.
    d. they can mutate back to a virulent strain.
    e. they usually require fewer boosters than other types of vaccines.

14. DNA vaccines where the microbial DNA is inserted into a plasmid vector and inoculated into a recipient are being hailed as the most promising of the newer approaches to immunization because animal studies have shown these vaccines to be safe and effective.
    a. True
    b. False

15. Vaccination is recommended for
    a. childhood diseases.
    b. health workers.
    c. travelers.
    d. military personnel.
    e. all of the above.

16. Titer is expressed as the highest dilution of serum that produces a visible reaction with an antigen.
    a. True
    b. False

17. The more a sample of serum can be diluted and yet still react with antigen, the lesser the concentration of antibodies in the sample and the higher the titer.
    a. True
    b. False

18. Complement fixation testing uses all of the following except
    a. antibody.
    b. antigen.
    c. sensitized human red blood cells.
    d. complement.
    e. sensitized sheep red blood cells.

19. If hemolysis does not occur, the result of the complement fixation test is negative.
    a. True
    b. False

20. *In vivo* serological testing involves subcutaneous injection of antigen to elicit a visible antigen-antibody response in the host.
    a. True
    b. False

17 Disorders in Immunity

OVERVIEW

The immune system protects the body against disease. When the immune system over reacts, the person may experience allergy or autoimmunity. Excessive immune response, hypersensitivity, is categorized into four groups: type I (atopy and anaphylaxis), type II (cytotoxic), type III (immune complex reactions), and type IV (delayed hypersensitivity reactions). When the immune system under reacts, the individual is immunodeficient from incomplete development, suppression, or destruction of the immune system.

I.   INTRODUCTION

Concept: The immune system is beneficial, protecting against disease; but it can also be detrimental when the immune response over reacts or under reacts.

II. TYPE I ALLERGIC REACTIONS: ATOPY AND ANAPHYLAXIS

Concept: Type I allergies are immediate in onset, associated with exposure to specific antigens, and recognized as atopy or anaphylaxis.

   Objective 1.   Discuss the two type I allergy subtypes (atopy and anaphylaxis) including epidemiology, routes of inoculation, mechanism of disease, and a description of specific syndromes.
   Objective 2.   Describe testing for and controlling allergies.

A.   List the factors that affect the outcome of allergy.

      Portals of allergen entry include:

Explain the significance of the sensitizing and provocative doses of allergen.

The antibody of allergy is _____.

The allergy antibody binds to mast cells and basophils. Upon a second or subsequent exposure to the allergen, these cells degranulate to release chemical mediators. Recall the effects of the following mediators:

histamine—

serotonin—

leukotrienes—

platelet-activating factor—

prostaglandins—

bradykinin—

Characterize these diseases:

hay fever—

asthma—

atopic dermatitis (eczema)—

food allergy—

drug allergy—

Contrast cutaneous and systemic anaphylaxis.

Anaphylactic response is greatly amplified as compared to atopic response. True/False

Matching.

____ *in vivo* method to detect precise atopic or anaphylactic sensitivities

____ difficult to pinpoint, false negatives and positives

____ *in vitro* measurement of allergen-specific IgE

    a. radioimmune assay serological testing

    b. skin testing

    c. food allergy

Summarize various methods of treating and preventing type I allergy:

avoidance of the allergen—

drugs that block the action of lymphocytes, mast cells, or mediators—

desensitization therapy—

III. TYPE II HYPERSENSITIVITIES: REACTIONS THAT LYSE FOREIGN CELLS

Concept: Type II hypersensitivities include transfusion reactions and autoimmunities involving complement-assisted lysis of cells by IgG and IgM directed against those cells' surface antigens.

    Objective 1. Explain the significance of genetically determined ABO isoantigens on red blood cells in blood typing, transfusions, and hemolytic disease of the newborn.

A. Matching.

____ most common blood type, neither A nor B RBC antigen, both anti-A and anti-B in serum

____ second most common blood type, A RBC antigen, anti-B in serum

____ third most common blood type, B RBC antigen, anti-A in serum

____ least common blood type, A and B RBC antigens, neither anti-A nor anti-B in serum

    a. type A

    b. type B

    c. type AB

    d. type O

A person with blood type O is called a _____.

A person with blood type AB is called a _____.

A person with blood type B can safely receive blood of which type(s)?

A person with blood type B can safely donate blood to persons of which type(s)?

A person possessing the rhesus monkey antigen on his/her red blood cells is said to be Rh _____.

A person who is Rh negative does not possess Rh antibodies against the Rh factor. These develop through:

Hemolytic disease of the newborn is a concern with second and subsequent pregnancies of an Rh negative mother who has previously given birth to an Rh positive fetus. Why?

How is prevention of hemolytic disease of the newborn accomplished?

IV. TYPE III HYPERSENSITIVITIES: IMMUNE COMPLEX REACTIONS

Concept: Similar to type II, type III hypersensitivities involve small antigens not attached to the cell surface that form large complexes when combined with antibodies.

Objective 1. Relate the mechanism of immune complex formation and the production of disease reactions to serum and vaccines.

A. Immune complexes are so abundant with type III hypersensitivity that they precipitate and become inaccessible to neutrophil phagocytosis. Then what happens?

V. AN INAPPROPRIATE RESPONSE AGAINST SELF: AUTOIMMUNITY

Concept: Autoimmune diseases are differentiated as systemic or organ-specific, and fall into the categories of type II or type III.

Objective 1. Explain the genetic and sexual correlation in autoimmune disease, as well as its origin.
Objective 2. Identify examples of autoimmune disease.

A. Susceptibility to autoimmune disease is influenced by genetics (cases cluster in families) and sex (afflicts _____ more than _____).

Review the theories on the origins of autoimmune disease:

sequestered antigen theory—

clonal selection theory—

122

immune deficiency theory—

B.   Fill in the chart.

Disease	Manifestations	Therapy
systemic lupus erythematosus		
rheumatoid arthritis		
Graves' disease		
Hashimoto's thyroiditis		
diabetes mellitus		
myasthenia gravis		
multiple sclerosis		

VI. TYPE IV HYPERSENSITIVITIES: CELL-MEDIATED (DELAYED) REACTIONS

Concept: Type IV diseases result when T cells act upon self tissues or transplanted foreign cells, with symptoms arising from one to several days following contact with the antigen.

   Objective 1.   Discuss the most common delayed allergic reaction—contact dermatitis.
   Objective 2.   Examine the concepts of graft rejection, tests for transplant compatibility, the reactions against grafts and their prevention, and the types of grafts.

A.   Outline the events of delayed hypersensitivity to poison ivy.

B.   In the more common case of the host rejecting a graft, a series of events occurs. Fill in the missing parts.

T cells of host recognize foreign class II MHC receptors on surface of grafted cells

$\downarrow$

T cells release _____

$\downarrow$

stimulus triggers cytotoxic T cells

$\downarrow$

cytotoxic T cells bind to grafted tissue and secrete _____
_____.

Late in the process, antibodies initiate _____ against the graft. Finally, the vascular supply is destroyed, promoting the death of the graft tissue. The less common graft rejection of host sometimes occurs when _____ is transplanted.

123

Matching.

___ transplant between genetically different individuals belonging to the same species

___ tissue transplanted from one site of an individual to another

___ transplant tissue from an identical twin

___ tissue transplant between individuals of different species

    a.   autograft
    b.   isograft
    c.   allograft
    d.   xenograft

To lessen the chance of tissue rejection, _____ typing and _____ typing are performed.

Even the best matches usually require drugs to suppress rejection. What characteristic of cyclosporine A warrants the label "miracle drug?"

List some of the more frequent transplants performed.

VII. IMMUNODEFICIENCY DISEASES: HYPOSENSITIVITY OF THE IMMUNE SYSTEM

Concept: Immunodeficiencies (stemming from genetic errors or caused by natural or artificial factors) result in recurrent, overwhelming infections, often with microbes that are not pathogenic to the immunocompetent person.

    Objective 1. Discuss the causes of the categories of primary and secondary immunodeficiency diseases.

A. Describe the mechanisms and symptoms of these disease processes.

B-cell deficiencies:

    agammaglobulinemia (hypogammaglobulinemia)—

    IgA deficiency—

T-cell deficiencies:

    DiGeorge syndrome—

    chronic mucocutaneous candidiasis—

B- and T-cell deficiencies: (severe combined immunodeficiencies):

    absence of lymphocyte stem cells in the marrow—

    dysfunction of B and T cells later in development—

adenosine deaminase deficiency—

List the general causal agents of acquired deficiencies in B and T cells, and provide an example of a disease resulting from each cause.

VIII. CANCER: CELLS OUT OF CONTROL

Concept: The study of cancer, named for the appendage-like projections that a spreading tumor develops, can be related to immunology.

Objective 1.   Characterize and classify cancers.
Objective 2.   Propose mechanisms for the development of cancer.
Objective 3.   Explain the function of the immune system in the case of cancer.

A.   Contrast benign and malignant cancers.

List four characteristics of cancer.

Define metastasis.

Contrast carcinomas and sarcomas.

B.   Site evidence for the interrelationship between genes and cancer.

Discuss the functions of proto-oncogenes, anti-oncogenes, and oncogenes as related to transformation.

Viruses and chromosomal damage (translocations, trisomies, whole chromosome losses, and deletions) appear to contribute to cancer development. Explain the method of stimulation for each of these contributors.

Contrast the mechanism of chemical and physical carcinogens.

C. List the primary types of cells that operate in surveillance and destruction of tumor cells.

What role do antibodies play in tumor destruction?

IX. SELF-TEST

1. These antigens originating outside the body elicit a hypersensitivity.
    a. endogenous
    b. exogenous
    c. self tissue
    d. immunoglobulins
    e. none of the above

2. The predisposition for type I allergies is inherited.
    a. True
    b. False

3. Allergens that enter by mouth are
    a. inhalants.
    b. injectants.
    c. ingestants.
    d. contactants.
    e. none of the above.

4. The ideal practice is to transfuse blood that is a perfect match (A to A, B to B) so cross matching prior to transfusion is not necessary.
    a. True
    b. False

5. A person with blood type AB+ could safely receive blood type(s)
    a. AB+, O+.
    b. AB-, O-.
    c. A+, B+.
    d. A-, B-.
    e. a and b.

6. Autoimmunity is
   a. hypersensitivity to self.
   b. hypersensitivity to endogenous antigens.
   c. hypersensitivity to exogenous antigens.
   d. a and b.
   e. a and c.

7. The skin sensitization test (delayed-type allergy to microorganisms) is used to diagnose all of the following infections *except*
   a. tuberculosis.
   b. syphilis.
   c. meningitis.
   d. histoplasmosis.
   e. toxoplasmosis.

8. When a donor's tissues display inherited surface receptors of a different MHC class, these cells of the recipient recognize its foreignness and react against it.
   a. T cells
   b. B cells
   c. macrophages
   d. neutrophils
   e. none of the above

9. A significant number of genetic B-cell deficiencies appear primarily in male children because they are
   a. Y-linked recessive traits.
   b. Y-linked dominant traits.
   c. X-linked dominant traits.
   d. X-linked recessive traits.
   e. none of the above.

10. Cancer rates vary according to
    a. age.
    b. geographic region.
    c. occupational exposure to carcinogens.
    d. diet.
    e. all of the above.

11. Atopy is any chronic local allergy (such as hay fever or asthma), whereas anaphylaxis is a systemic, often explosive reaction that involves airway obstruction and circulatory collapse.
    a. True
    b. False

12. Factors that affect the presence of type I allergy include
    a. genetic predisposition.
    b. age.
    c. infection.
    d. geographic locale.
    e. all of the above.

13. The initial encounter with an allergen provides the provocative dose that primes the immune system for a subsequent encounter with that allergen but generally elicits no signs or symptoms.
    a. True
    b. False

14. Cytokines (such as histamine, serotonin, and leukotriene), secreted by macrophages and monocytes, give rise to numerous local and systemic reactions.
    a. True
    b. False

15. The most common food allergens include all except
    a. peanuts.
    b. fish.
    c. cow's milk.
    d. goat's milk.
    e. eggs.

16. Cutaneous anaphylaxis is inflammation to the local injection of allergen, whereas systemic anaphylaxis is characterized by sudden respiratory and circulatory disruption that can be fatal in a few minutes.
    a. True
    b. False

17. Therapy to counteract allergens includes
    a. antihistamines.
    b. epinephrine.
    c. aspirin and acetaminophen.
    d. desensitization through controlled injections of specific allergens.
    e. all of the above.

18. Examples of autoimmune diseases include all except
    a. systemic lupus erythematosus.
    b. rheumatoid arthritis.
    c. heart disease.
    d. diabetes mellitus.
    e. multiple sclerosis.

19. Immunodeficiencies are categorized as either primary diseases, present at birth (usually stemming from genetic errors), or secondary diseases, acquired after birth (caused by natural or artificial agents).
    a. True
    b. False

20. Which type of graft is least likely to be rejected?
    a. xenograft
    b. allograft
    c. autograft
    d. isograft
    e. none of the above

Introduction to Identification Techniques in Medical Bacteriology

OVERVIEW

Successful identification and treatment depends on how specimens are collected, handled, and stored. Following collection of a sample, a variety of methods may be employed to identify the infectious agent. Flow charts and/or diagnostic tables used with the information gained from the various identification methods can help pinpoint the genus and species that fits a particular combination of characteristics.

I. INTRODUCTION

Concept: Various methods are used to collect, isolate, and identify infectious agents.

II. ON THE TRACK OF THE INFECTIOUS AGENT: SPECIMEN COLLECTION

Concept: Isolation and identification through microscopic, physiological, serological, and other tests are important to the diagnosis of disease.

> **Objective 1.** Discuss specimen collection.
> **Objective 2.** Explain specimen analysis through immediate direct tests, general, and specific tests employed in cultivation of the specimen.

A. Who may collect specimens?

What is the importance of aseptic or sterile sampling procedures?

B. Contrast presumptive and confirmatory tests.

Direct tests are rapid and do not require cultivation of the specimen. List some of these techniques.

List three general types of media used for microbial isolation.

Biochemical tests check for the presence or absence of an _____, which catalyzes the microbial conversion of the substrate into the end product.

Describe the use of flow charts to identify bacteria, include the advantage and disadvantage of this procedure.

List the criteria for determining the clinical significance of cultures.

III. SELF-TEST

1. Where should the specimen be stored until it can be manipulated at some later time?
   a. on the lab bench
   b. in the refrigerator
   c. in the incubator
   d. at the nurses' station
   e. none of the above

2. Isolated colonies are desirable; working with mixed or contaminated cultures is fraught with problems.
   a. True
   b. False

3. Besides morphological and biochemical tests, all of the following may be employed in bacterial identification *except*
   a. serotyping.
   b. antimicrobic sensitivity.
   c. phage typing.
   d. Gram staining.
   e. gene probing.

4. Throat swabs should touch the tongue, cheeks, and saliva for best results.
   a. True
   b. False

5. Swab sample transport systems contain nonnutritive maintenance media, so the microbes do not grow.
   a. True
   b. False

6. Test results that provide presumptive data
   a. isolate the microbe.
   b. kill the microbe.
   c. place the microbe in a preliminary category such as genus.
   d. place the microbe based on definitive evidence in a species.
   e. all of the above.

7. Isolation media include
   a. enriched media.
   b. selective media.
   c. differential media.
   d. blood agar.
   e. all of the above.

8. In biochemical testing, what indicates that a particular enzyme is expressed in a certain species?
   a. the presence of the enzyme in the medium
   b. the presence of the substrate in the medium
   c. the presence of ATP in the medium
   d. the presence of a particular end product in the medium with a special substrate
   e. none of the above

9 Antimicrobic sensitivity is used
   a. in determining the drugs to be used in treatment.
   b. in presumptive identification of *Streptococcus*.
   c. as selective agents in many media.
   d. in presumptive identification of *Clostridium*.
   e. in all of the above.

10. Problems in determining the clinical significance of cultures include:
   a. Is an isolate clinically important?
   b. Is an isolate a contaminant or just part of the normal flora?
   c. Is the pathogen a different species than that in the normal flora?
   d. Is the pathogen more virulent than the normal flora?
   e. all of the above.

18   The Cocci of Medical Importance

OVERVIEW

The cocci of medical importance belong to the *Staphylococcus* and *Streptococcus* genera and the family Neisseriaceae. Most of the staphylococci are human commensals, but some are pathogenic. Both staphylococci and streptococci are becoming difficult to treat because of developing resistance to antimicrobic drugs. While most Neisseriaceae are commensals causing opportunistic infections, *Neisseria gonorrhoeae* and *meningitidis* are significant pathogens.

I.   INTRODUCTION

Concept: The cocci are among the most significant agents of human disease.

II.   GENERAL CHARACTERISTICS OF THE STAPHYLOCOCCI

Concept: *Staphylococcus* is one of three genera of cocci involved in infectious disease in humans.

Objective 1.   Characterize and give the common habitat of the members of the genus *Staphylococcus*.
Objective 2.   Relate the properties of *Staphylococcus aureus* contributing to its resistance and pathogenicity.
Objective 3.   Discuss the carriage of *S. aureus*.
Objective 4.   Describe staphylococcal infections, both localized and toxigenic.
Objective 5.   Recall host defenses against *S. aureus*.
Objective 6.   Propose methods for the identification of *S. aureus*.
Objective 7.   Explain how the antibiotic resistance of *S. aureus* makes the treatment of infections challenging and, as a result, encourages methods of prevention.

A.   Where are staphylococcal organisms generally found?

Describe the staphylococcal cells:

shape—

arrangement—

gram reaction—

presence or absence of other morphological structures—

B. List the properties of *S. aureus* that make it the most resistant of all non-spore-forming pathogens.

Describe the mechanism of these virulence factors associated with *S. aureus:*

coagulase—

hemolysins—

leukocidins—

enterotoxins—

exfoliative—

C. Healthy carriers intermittently harbor *S. aureus* in the:

Indicate predisposing conditions to *S. aureus* infection.

Nosocomial infections with *S. aureus* are a problem in what areas of the hospital?

D. *Staphylococcus* enter the skin through:

Contrast furuncles and carbuncles.

Name some foods that, when contaminated by handling and then left unrefrigerated for a few hours, may induce staphylococcal food poisoning.

Detail the action of the food-poisoning toxin on the body and the response of the body.

E. The antibodies to the staphylococcal antigens do not seem to provide long-lasting protection. The most powerful defense lies in the phagocytic response by _____ and _____.

F. What media are used for staphylococcal isolation?

Which biochemical test differentiates staphylococci from streptococci?

Which biochemical test differentiates *S. aureus* from *Staphylococcus epidermidis?*

G. Name some of the drugs to which *S. aureus* demonstrates a resistance or tolerance.

Outline several methods used to prevent *S. aureus* contamination which could result in an infection.

III. GENERAL CHARACTERISTICS OF THE STREPTOCOCCI AND RELATED GENERA

Concept: Streptococci are normal flora and agents of disease in humans.

Objective 1. Characterize and classify the streptococci.
Objective 2. Enumerate some of the factors contributing to the virulence of group A, ß-hemolytic streptococci.
Objective 3. Discuss the epidemiology of the various types of *S. pyogenes* infections.
Objective 4. Describe identification of the streptococci.
Objective 5. Characterize the diseases of other streptococci, their transmission, and treatment.

A. Give a general description of streptococci:

arrangement—

shape—

presence or absence of other morphological structures—

Contrast the Lancefield classification system and the division of species based upon reaction on blood agar.

B. Indicate how each of the following contributes to the virulence of group A streptococci:

C-carbohydrates—

M-proteins—

streptolysins—

erythrogenic toxin—

streptokinase—

hyaluronidase—

C. Matching.

____ delayed inflammatory condition of the joints and heart
____ secondary to influenza
____ tonsillitis, swollen cervical lymph nodes
____ burning, itchy papules associated with insect bites,
      poor hygiene, and crowded living conditions
____ high fever with red diffuse rash
____ edema and redness of skin near small wound or
      incision, spreads outward
____ complication usually limited to persons in weakened
      condition
____ disease of the kidney, thought to be the result of
      autoimmune response to various streptococcal antigens

a. pyoderma
b. erysipelas
c. pharyngitis
d. scarlet fever
e. septicemia
f. pneumonia
g. rheumatic fever
h. acute glomerulonephritis

What host defenses provide long-term protection from *S. pyogenes?*

D. Identify the organism described by each group of lab tests.

_____ gram + cocci in chains, catalase –, ß hemolytic on blood agar,
                          positive bacitracin disc test
_____ gram + cocci in chains, catalase –, α hemolytic
_____ gram + cocci in chains, catalase –, tolerant to heat and 6.5% salt
                          and resistant to low concentrations of penicillin G
_____ gram + cocci in pairs or short chains, large capsules,
                          α hemolytic on blood, growth improved by 5–10% carbon
                          dioxide
_____ gram + cocci in chains, catalase –, optochin +, bile solubility +,
                          inulin fermentation +

E.   Identify the causative organism.

_____   located in the vagina and transferred to the infant during the delivery, implicated in neonatal infections

_____   normal colonists of human large intestine, infections arise most often in the elderly undergoing surgery or otherwise predisposed

_____   constant inhabitants of gums or teeth, dental procedures can lead to infection, with the most important complication being subacute endocarditis

_____   causes dental carries

_____   encapsulated organism causes pneumonia particularly favored by the factors of old age, winter season, weakened lungs/defenses, institutional lifestyle

What is the antibiotic of choice for treating streptococcal infections?

IV. THE FAMILY NEISSERIACEAE: GRAM-NEGATIVE COCCI AND COCCOBACILLI

Concept: Members of the Neisseriaceae are relatively innocuous residents of the mucous membranes of warm-blooded animals.

Objective 1.   Characterize the genus *Neisseria* and differentiate the pathogenic and nonpathogenic species.

Objective 2.   Describe the transmission, infection, diagnosis, treatment, and prevention of *N. gonorrhoeae.*

Objective 3.   Describe the transmission, infection, diagnosis, treatment, and prevention of *N. meningitidis.*

Objective 4.   Discuss some of the other gram-negative cocci and coccobacilli.

A.   Describe the genus *Neisseria:*

cell shape—

cell arrangement—

gram reaction—

presence or absence of other morphological structures—

oxygen requirements—

oxidase enzyme (produced or not produced)—

What additional tests are useful in differentiating pathogenic from nonpathogenic *Neisseria?*

B. Transmission of *N. gonorrhoeae* is through _____ contact.

Contrast gonococcal infections in males, females, and children.

How is gonorrhea diagnosed?

Detail two accepted treatment regimens for gonococcal infections.

Outline methods for control of the spread of gonorrhea.

C. Summarize the occurrence, carriage, and transmission of *N. meningitidis.*

List the symptoms of meningitis.

How is meningococcal meningitis diagnosed?

Most individuals have a well-developed _____ immunity to meningococcal meningitis.

What is the antibiotic of choice to treat meningococcal meningitis?

D. What laboratory tests are used to distinguish *Branhamella catarrhalis* (which causes meningitis, endocarditis, otitis media, bronchopulmonary infections, and neonatal conjunctivitis) from *Neisseria?*

Treatment of *Moraxella* infections is by which antibiotic(s)?

Acinetobacter, found in soil, water, and sewage, ordinarily is not clinically significant. In rare cases it has been associated with _____ infection, affecting traumatized or debilitated persons.

V.   SELF-TEST

1.   Normal flora includes the staphylococci of the mucous membranes and
   a.   ear.
   b.   pancreas.
   c.   intestines.
   d.   skin.
   e.   blood.

2.   *Neisseria meningitidis* is usually the cause of meningitis in
   a.   neonates.
   b.   preschool children.
   c.   elementary school children and young adults.
   d.   middle-age individuals.
   e.   senior citizens.

3.   Infection with *Streptococcus pneumoniae* can be prevented in high risk individuals by
   a.   vaccine.
   b.   prophylactic antibiotic therapy.
   c.   vitamin C.
   d.   both a and b.
   e.   none of the above.

4.   Toxic shock syndrome is a disease process caused by a toxin produced by
   a.   *Neisseria gonorrhoeae.*
   b.   *Streptococcus pyogenes.*
   c.   *Staphylococcus aureus.*
   d.   *Staphylococcus epidermidis.*
   e.   *Staphylococcus saprophyticus.*

5.   Most systemic staphylococcal infections begin as local cutaneous infections, then enter the blood to travel to the
   a.   bones.
   b.   lungs.
   c.   kidneys.
   d.   heart.
   e.   all of the above.

6.   Infections with *S. pyogenes* are generally transmitted through all the following means *except*
   a.   direct contact.
   b.   air.
   c.   a droplet.
   d.   food.
   e.   fomites.

7.   Serological tests revealing anti-streptococcal antibodies are not prompt enough for diagnosis; instead, the tests are mainly used to detect continuing or recent infection.
   a.   True
   b.   False

8.   Streptococcal infections include
   a.   pneumonia.
   b.   otitis media.
   c.   endocarditis.
   d.   septicemia.
   e.   all of the above.

9.   Extragenital gonococcal infections never occur.
   a.   True
   b.   False

10.   Responses to gonococcal infections produce a lasting immunity, so one need not worry about recurrent infections.
   a.   True
   b.   False

11.   It is impossible to carry a pathogen such as *Staphylococcus aureus* without any symptoms.
   a.   True
   b.   False

12. Staphylococci produce the enzyme catalase that breaks down hydrogen peroxide accumulated during oxidative metabolism, whereas streptococci do not.
    a. True
    b. False

13. The term for complete hemolysis on blood agar is alpha hemolysis.
    a. True
    b. False

14. Impetigo
    a. is caused by group A streptococci.
    b. is caused by staphylococci.
    c. is characterized by the skin peeling, separating the epidermal layer from the dermis.
    d. is a localized form of scalded skin syndrome.
    e. is all of the above.

15. Since staphylococci rarely acquire drug resistance, pencillin is the drug of choice for treatment of all staphylococcal infections.
    a. True
    b. False

16. *Streptococcus pyogenes* causes
    a. erysipelas.
    b. scarlet fever.
    c. strep throat (pharyngitis).
    d. pyoderma.
    e. all of the above.

17. *Streptococcus pneumoniae* can cause otitis media.
    a. True
    b. False

18. *Streptococcus pneumoniae* is beta hemolytic.
    a. True
    b. False

19. *Acinetobacter* is commonly found in soil and water and is increasingly isolated in nosocomial infections.
    a. True
    b. False

20. Staphylococcal food poisoning is associated with eating all of the following foods except
    a. custards.
    b. cream pastries.
    c. chicken salad.
    d. hamburger patties.
    e. sauces.

19   The Gram-Positive Bacilli of Medical Importance

OVERVIEW

The gram positive bacilli are separated into groups based on the presence or absence of endospores and the characteristic of acid-fastness. The endospore-forming gram positive bacilli include highly toxigenic and virulent pathogens. Non-endospore forming, non-acid fast, gram positive bacilli include those organisms that cause listeriosis and diptheria. Non-endospore forming, acid-fast organisms include those that cause recurring tuberculosis and leprosy, as seen in ancient times.

I.   INTRODUCTION

Concept: Bacilli are responsible for many ancient diseases such as leprosy, as well as many newly emerging diseases such as listeriosis.

II.   GRAM-POSITIVE, SPORE-FORMING BACILLI

Concept: The genera *Bacillus, Clostridium,* and *Sporolactobacillus* form spores that are resistant to heat, drying, radiation, and chemicals.

Objective 1.   Characterize the genus *Bacillus,* including metabolism and habitat.
Objective 2.   Discuss the medically important members of the genus *Bacillus.*
Objective 3.   Characterize the genus *Clostridium,* including metabolism and habitat.
Objective 4.   Discuss the medically important members of the genus *Clostridium.*

A.   Identify the characteristics of *Bacillus:*

oxygen requirements—

catalase—

cell shape—

metabolism (including beneficial by-products)—

habitat—

B.   Outline the cycle of vegetative growth and sporulation of *B. anthracis.*

What persons are at risk of contracting anthrax from domesticated livestock?

List and describe the forms of anthrax.

Describe the methods for the control of anthrax.

Propose a scenario for intoxication by *B. cereus*.

C.   Identify the characteristics of *Clostridium:*

oxygen requirements—

catalase—

cell shape—

metabolism (including beneficial by-products)—

habitat—

D.   Outline the cycle of spore germination and vegetative growth of *C. perfringens.*

Contrast anaerobic cellulitis and myonecrosis.

Describe methods for treatment and prevention of infection by *C. perfringens.*

Detail the cause, occurrence, symptoms, treatment, and prevention of *C. difficile.*

Relate the details for infection with *C. tetani.*

What is the most common cause of death in patients infected with *C. tetani?*

Describe methods for treatment and prevention of *C. tetani.*

Fill in the chart, comparing the types of clostridial food poisoning.

Organism	Foods most frequently involved	Onset time of symptoms	Symptoms	Treatment	Prevention
C. perfringens					
C. botulinum					

III. GRAM-POSITIVE, REGULAR, NON-SPORE-FORMING RODS

Concept: *Listeria monocytogenes* and *Erysipelothrix rhusiopathiae* are non-spore-forming rods classified as regular because of a tendency to stain uniformly and not to assume pleomorphic shapes.

 Objective 1. Characterize *L. monocytogenes*—the organism, transmission, infection, treatment, and prevention.
 Objective 2. Characterize *E. rhusiopathiae*—the organism, transmission, infection, treatment, and prevention.

A. Describe these characteristics of *L. monocytogenes:*

cell shape—

cell arrangement—

metabolism—

reservoir—

transmission—

symptoms—

treatment—

prevention—

142

B.   Describe these characteristics of *E. rhusiopathiae:*

cell shape—

reservoir—

transmission—

symptoms—

treatment—

prevention—

IV. GRAM-POSITIVE, IRREGULAR, NON-SPORE-FORMING RODS

Concept: *Corynebacterium* are non-spore-forming rods classified as irregular because of a tendency to stain unevenly and to possess pleomorphic shapes.

Objective 1.   Characterize *C. diptheriae*—the organism, transmission, infection, treatment, and prevention.

A.   Describe these characteristics of *C. diptheriae:*

cell shape—

cell arrangement—

reservoir—

transmission—

symptoms of infection—

symptoms of localized inflammation and toxemia—

treatment—

prevention—

V.   MYCOBACTERIA: ACID-FAST BACILLI

Concept: Many persons worldwide are afflicted with these acid-fast, resistant, filamentous or branching, slow growing rods called mycobacteria.

Objective 1.   Discuss susceptibility factors and transmission of tuberculosis (TB).
Objective 2.   Characterize tuberculosis infection, identification, treatment, and prevention.

Objective 3. Characterize *M. leprae*—the organism, transmission, infection, treatment, and prevention.

Objective 4. Describe infections caused by mycobacteria, other than tuberculosis and leprosy.

A. List the personal factors contributing to an individual's susceptibility to TB.

Recall how TB is transmitted.

B. Outline the course of untreated TB.

Contrast the following:

primary TB infection—

secondary TB infection—

extrapulmonary TB—

Summarize the techniques involved in the clinical diagnosis of TB.

Describe the treatment for TB, including the drugs of choice and the considerations for the selection of the therapeutic agent(s).

Review the procedure(s) for the prevention of TB.

C. Indicate the exceptional characteristics of *M. leprae.*

Though the mechanism of transmission of *M. leprae* is not yet verified, list several predisposing or contributing factors for the transmission of this organism.

Outline the course of infection, including the time of incubation, for leprosy.

Contrast the following:

tuberculoid leprosy—

lepromatous leprosy—

borderline leprosy—

Summarize the techniques involved in the clinical diagnosis of leprosy.

Briefly discuss the treatment and prevention of leprosy.

D. Relate the persons affected, method(s) of transmission, and symptoms of disease for these organisms:

M. avium-intracellulare—

M. kansasii—

M. fortuitum—

M. marinum—

M. scrofulaceum—

VI. SELF-TEST

1. Though the incidence of tetanus in North America is low, most cases occur in
    a. geriatric patients.
    b. intravenous drug abusers.
    c. neonates.
    d. a and b.
    e. a and c.

2. Botulism in the U.S. is associated with which of the following foods?
    a. home-canned green beans
    b. home-canned corn
    c. home-cured meats
    d. home-cured fish
    e. all of the above

3. Myonecrosis, caused by gas gangrene that has spread into healthy tissue, may be the result of an infection with
    a. *Clostridium perfringens.*
    b. *Clostridium botulinum.*
    c. *Clostridium tenani.*
    d. *Bacillus cereus.*
    e. *Bacillus subtilis.*

4. The organism identified in question three also causes
    a. food poisoning.
    b. neuromuscular disturbances.
    c. lock-jaw.
    d. colitis.
    e. tremors.

5. Listeriosis in adults is most often a mild or subclinical infection with nonspecific symptoms (fever, diarrhea, sore throat), while a high mortality rate is associated with fetuses and neonates.
   a. True
   b. False

6. Listeriosis is usually associated with ingesting contaminated
   a. fruits.
   b. vegetables.
   c. dairy products.
   d. all of the above.
   e. none of the above.

7. Diphtheria can be an infection of
   a. the skin.
   b. the respiratory tract.
   c. toxins directed toward the heart.
   d. all of the above.
   e. none of the above.

8. Humans are easily infected with the tubercle bacillus and quite readily develop the disease.
   a. True
   b. False

9. A positive tuberculin skin test is all the evidence needed to diagnose a case of tuberculosis.
   a. True
   b. False

10. Leprosy is a chronic, progressive disease of the skin and nerves that is not readily communicated.
    a. True
    b. False

11. The treatment for gas gangrene that is least effective is
    a. surgery.
    b. vaccination.
    c. debridement.
    d. antibiotics.
    e. cleansing the area.

12. The primary lesion of tuberculosis is usually a tubercle in the
    a. lung.
    b. liver.
    c. skin.
    d. kidney.
    e. heart.

13. *Clostridium perfringens* are
    a. non-sporeforming aerobes.
    b. spore-forming aerobes.
    c. non-sporeforming anaerobes.
    d. spore-forming anaerobes.
    e. none of the above.

14. Treatment for tetanus is accomplished with muscle relaxants, antibiotics, and
    a. immunization.
    b. antifungal medication.
    c. antiviral medication.
    d. antibodies.
    e. antitoxin.

15. Tetanus organisms grow on vital, healthy tissue.
    a. True
    b. False

16. Heat can inactivate botulism toxin, but cannot kill the organisms that produce the toxin.
    a. True
    b. False

17. New cases of tuberculosis in the United States are decreasing because of conditions such as AIDS.
    a. True
    b. False

18. Treatment for tuberculosis involves a ten day course of antibiotics, hydration therapy, and bed rest.
    a. True
    b. False

19. Predisposing factors for contracting
    tuberculosis include
    a.   poor nutritional status.
    b.   poverty.
    c.   unclean living conditions.
    d.   compromised immune system.
    e.   all of the above.

20. *Mycobacterium leprae* has a relatively long
    incubation period.
    a.   True
    b.   False

20 The Gram-Negative Bacilli of Medical Importance

OVERVIEW

The medically important gram-negative bacilli include aerobes and facultative anaerobes. The aerobes include the genera *Pseudomonas*, *Brucella*, *Francisella*, *Bordetella*, and *Legionella*. The facultative anaerobes include the families Enterobacteriaceae and Pasteurellaceae. The oxidase-negative Enterobacteriaceae includes both enterics and nonenterics. The oxidase-positive Pasteurellaceae includes both the genera *Pasteurella* and *Hemophilus*.

I. INTRODUCTION

Concept: The gram-negative bacilli are a large and complex group, many of which are not medically important.

II. AEROBIC GRAM-NEGATIVE NONENTERIC BACILLI

Concept: The gram-negative bacilli which are medically important can be subdivided into genera that are opportunists and genera of frank (true) pathogens.

> **Objective 1.** Characterize and discuss the medical importance of selected aerobic gram-negative bacteria.

A. Describe these characteristics of *Pseudomonas aeruginosa:*

habitat—

conditions predisposing a person to infection—

complications of infection—

odor—

color of fluorescent pigment produced—

drugs used to treat infection—

Describe these characteristics of *Brucella:*

persons at risk of infection—

transmission—

symptoms—

drugs used to treat infection—

prevention—

Describe these characteristics of *Francisella tularensis:*

reservoir—

vectors—

transmission—

symptoms—

drugs used to treat infection—

prevention—

Describe these characteristics of *Bordetella pertussis:*

reservoir—

transmission—

symptoms of catarrhal stage—

symptoms of paroxysmal stage—

prevention—

Describe these characteristics of *Legionella:*

cell shape—

nutritional requirements—

habitat—

transmission—

symptoms—

drugs used to treat infection—

III. IDENTIFICATION AND DIFFERENTIAL CHARACTERISTICS OF THE ENTEROBACTERIACEAE

Concept: This large family of gram-negative rods is divided into: the enteric pathogens, including the lactose-fermenting coliforms and the non-lactose-fermenting noncoliforms, which are responsible for severe diarrheal illnesses and 50% of all nosocomial infections; and the nonenteric pathogens which are not associated with the gastrointestinal tract nor with diseases of the gastrointestinal tract.

Objective 1. Characterize the members of the family Enterobacteriaceae.
Objective 2. Discuss the coliforms and related diseases.
Objective 3. Discuss the noncoliforms and related diseases.
Objective 4. Characterize *Yersinia pestis* and its association with the plague.
Objective 5. Characterize *Pasteurella* and the concerns of infection.
Objective 6. Characterize *Hemophilus* species and diseases.

A. Fill in the missing steps for isolating and identifying the oxidase-negative, catalase-positive, non-spore-forming, straight, gram-negative rods.

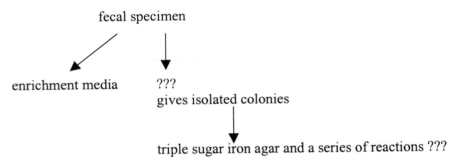

List the complex surface antigens, inducing antibody formation important to serological testing, that correspond to the designations:

H—
K—
O—

B. *Escherichia coli* is mistakenly viewed as a harmless commensal of the human intestine, but various strains are either true or opportunistic pathogens. Relate the transmission, complications, and treatment of these diseases associated with *E. coli* infection:

infantile diarrhea—

traveler's diarrhea—

urinary tract infections—

Explain the rationale for using *E. coli* (coliforms) to test water and dairy products for fecal contamination.

Briefly discuss these coliforms as they relate to disease:

Klebsiella—

Enterobacter—

Citrobacter—

Serratia—

Describe these characteristics of *Proteus:*

habitat—

appearance of growth on the surface of moist agar—

diseases resulting from infection—

C. Describe these characteristics of *Salmonella typhi:*

transmission of typhoid fever—

symptoms of typhoid fever—

drugs used to treat typhoid fever—

Describe these characteristics of nontyphoidal salmonelloses:

reservoir—

transmission—

symptoms of disease—

treatment of disease—

Contrast salmonellosis and shigellosis; include transmission, infecting dose, and production of disease.

D. Describe these characteristics of plague:

virulence factors of *Y. pestis*—

persons at risk—

transmission—

treatment of disease—

prevention of disease—

Outline the cycle for the spread of *Y. pestis*.

Contrast bubonic, septicemic, and pneumonic plague.

E. List some of the animal hosts for *P. multocida*.

How is this zoonotic disease transmitted to humans?

Describe the disease process in humans.

F. *Hemophilus* requires X and V factors for growth. How are these factors supplied in artificial media?

Fill in the chart.

Organism	Disease	Transmission	Symptoms	Treatment
H. influenzae				
H. aegyptius				
H. ducreyi				

IV. SELF-TEST

1. An infection occurring as a result of medical treatment.
   a. infectious
   b. nosocomial
   c. iatrogenic
   d. asymptomatic
   e. abnormal

2. Which of the following is an opportunistic pathogen?
   a. *Pseudomonas* sp.
   b. *Brucella* sp.
   c. *Bordetella* sp.
   d. *Legionella* sp.
   e. *Francisella* sp.

3. Which of the following is (are) zoonotic disease(s)?
   a. *Pseudomonas* infection
   b. brucellosis
   c. pertussis
   d. legionellosis
   e. all of the above

4. Sponges should be cleaned and allowed to dry between uses to avoid skin rash caused by
   a. *Pseudomonas* sp.
   b. *Brucella* sp.
   c. *Bordetella* sp.
   d. *Legionella* sp.
   e. *Francisella* sp.

5. *Brucella abortus* causes abortion in cattle and humans.
   a. True
   b. False

6. Which of the following appears to be widely distributed in aqueous habitats and causes pneumonia?
   a. *Pseudomonas* sp.
   b. *Brucella* sp.
   c. *Bordetella* sp.
   d. *Legionella* sp.
   e. *Francisella* sp.

7. Coliforms include all except
   a. *E. coli.*
   b. *Klebsiella pneumoniae.*
   c. *Enterobacter* sp.
   d. *Shigella flexneri.*
   e. *Serratia marcescens.*

8. The IMViC tests include
   a. inositol, methyl red, Voges-Proskauer, citrate.
   b. inositol, mannitol, Voges-Proskauer, citrate.
   c. indole, methyl red, Voges-Proskauer, citrate.
   d. indole, mannitol, Voges-Proskauer, citrate.
   e. none of the above.

9. Organisms implicated in the diagnosis of bloody diarrhea include
   a. *E. coli.*
   b. *Entamoeba histolytica.*
   c. *Salmonella enteriditis.*
   d. *Shigella flexneri.*
   e. all of the above.

10. Vaccination with Hib vaccine is recommended for
    a. everyone.
    b. elementary school children.
    c. children entering day care.
    d. teenagers.
    e. adults.

11. *Salmonella* are normal flora in the intestines of
    a. only chickens.
    b. only humans.
    c. no animal.
    d. cattle, poultry, rodents and reptiles.
    e. none of the above.

12. *Bordetella pertusis* causes
    a. rabies.
    b. necrosis.
    c. whooping cough.
    d. undulant fever.
    e. all of the above.

13. Which organism produces a red pigment and causes pneumonia?
    a. *Salmonella*
    b. *Citrobacter*
    c. *Enterobacter*
    d. *Serratia*
    e. *Klebsiella*

14. *Hemophilus influenzae* requires a vector for transmission.
    a. True
    b. False

15. *E. coli* are used to detect fecal contamination of milk and water because
    a. they are gram-negative and easy to find.
    b. they grow well under artificial conditions.
    c. they are present in hamburger meat.
    d. they are normally found in the intestines of warm-blooded animals.
    e. all of the above.

16. Bubonic plague is transmitted by which of the following vectors?
    a. rats
    b. flies
    c. mosquitoes
    d. ticks
    e. fleas

17. Traveler's diarrhea is most likely caused by
    a. *Amoeba*.
    b. *Shigella*.
    c. *E. coli*.
    d. *Salmonella*.
    e. *Giardia*.

18. True pathogens include all except:
    a. *Salmonella*.
    b. *Yersinia pestis*.
    c. *Bordetella*.
    d. *Brucella*.
    e. *Pseudomonas*.

19. Many species of this genus produce pigments (green, brown, red, or yellow) that diffuse into the medium and change its color.
    a. *E. coli*
    b. *Serratia*
    c. *Pseudomonas*
    d. *Pasteurella*
    e. *Klebsiella*

20. With an infectious dose of 10–50 organisms, *Francisella tularensis* is often considered one of the most infectious of all bacteria.
    a. True
    b. False

21 Miscellaneous Bacterial Agents of Disease

OVERVIEW

Bacteria that do not fit within the usual groups (rods and cocci) include the spirochetes, curved bacteria, short spirals, obligate intracellular organisms, and those bacteria that lack a cell wall. Many of these bacteria are transmitted to humans by such vectors as ticks, lice, and fleas. Also included in this chapter are bacteria associated with dental diseases.

I. INTRODUCTION

Concept: Several bacteria that cause infections are not the usual gram-positive or gram-negative rods or cocci.

II. THE SPIROCHETES

Concept: The spirochetes are gram-negative, helical bacteria with internal flagella (axial filament) endowing them with a distinctive mode of locomotion.

Objective 1. Characterize the genus *Treponema,* particularly as it relates to syphilis.
Objective 2. Characterize the genus *Leptospira* and the disease caused by this organism.
Objective 3. Characterize *Borrelia* as it relates to relapsing fever and Lyme disease.

A. Describe these characteristics of *T. pallidum:*

habitat—

oxygen requirements—

transmission—

target tissues—

generation time—

Relate the details of:

primary syphilis—

secondary syphilis—

latency syphilis—

tertiary syphilis—

congenital syphilis—

Explain the use of dark-field microscopy and serology for diagnosing syphilis.

What is the drug of choice for treating syphilis?

What is the most important aspect in the prevention of syphilis?

B. Which species of *Leptospira* causes disease in humans and animals?

How is this species distinguished from the other harmless free-living saprobes?

Describe these characteristics of leptospirosis:

reservoir—

transmission—

target tissues—

early phase—

second (immune) phase—

diagnosis—

treatment—

prevention—

C. Fill in the chart regarding relapsing fever.

	B. hermsii	B. recurrentis
arthropod vector		
reservoir		
persons at risk		
early symptoms		
later symptoms		
recovery		
diagnosis		
treatment		
prevention		

B. burgdorferi, responsible for Lyme disease, is transmitted by _____.

Outline the life cycle of this organism as it involves two principal hosts.

Describe these characteristics of Lyme disease:

early symptoms—

later symptoms—

persons at risk—

peak seasons—

treatment—

prevention—

III. OTHER CURVIFORM GRAM-NEGATIVE BACTERIA OF MEDICAL IMPORTANCE

Concept: The family Vibrionaceae includes the genus *Vibrio* (curved rods), while the family Spirillaceae includes the genera *Campylobacter* (short spirals) and *Spirillum* (inflexible coiled rods).

Objective 1. Characterize these diseases of the genus *Vibrio:* cholera and gastroenteritis.
Objective 2. Characterize the diseases caused by *C. jejuni* and *C. fetus.*

A. Describe these characteristics of cholera:

carrier state—

transmission—

outbreaks—

symptoms—

supportive therapy and treatment—

prevention—

Review the mechanism of the cholera toxin on intestinal cells.

Propose a scenario for the contraction, development of symptoms, treatment, and control of parahemolyticus gastroenteritis.

B. Differentiate between the diseases caused by *C. jejuni* and *C. fetus.*

IV. MEDICALLY IMPORTANT BACTERIA OF UNIQUE MORPHOLOGY AND BIOLOGY

Concept: The rickettsias and chlamydias have an atypical morphology and mode of existence.

Objective 1. Characterize the rickettsias and their association with disease.
Objective 2. Characterize the chlamydias and their association with disease.

A. Explain why the rickettsias were at one time thought to be related to viruses.

Rickettsias are generally transmitted by vectors. Identify the various methods of transmission of the different vectors:

ticks and mites—

fleas and lice—

List the general pathologic effects of rickettsial infection.

Fill in the chart.

	Causal organism	Transmission	Incidence	Manifestations	Treatment	Prevention
epidemic, louse-borne typhus						
endemic, flea-borne typhus						
scrub typhus						
Rocky Mt. spotted fever						
cat-scratch disease						
Q fever						

B.   Describe the two distinct stages of the chlamydias:

elementary body—

reticulate body—

Contrast the chlamydial diseases of the eye—ocular trachoma and inclusion conjunctivitis.

Discuss the sexually transmitted chlamydial diseases.

A chlamydial disease transmitted through the air to humans by birds, with symptoms similar to influenza and pneumococcal pneumonia is _____.

V. MOLLICUTES AND OTHER CELL-WALL-DEFICIENT BACTERIA

Concept: The smallest self-replicating microorganisms lacking a cell wall are the mycoplasmas.

Objective 1. Characterize *Mycoplasma* and its association with disease.

A. Recall the reason for the pleomorphism of *Mycoplasma*.

Explain why mycoplasma infections are chronic and difficult to eliminate.

Discuss the basis for the nickname "walking pneumonia" as it applies to atypical mycoplasmal pneumonia.

VI. BACTERIA IN DENTAL DISEASES

Concept: The mouth is a small-scale ecosystem with a diversity of surfaces for colonization and an ample supply of food.

Objective 1. Discuss the role of microorganisms in hard tissue disease of the mouth.
Objective 2. Discuss the role of microorganisms in soft tissue disease of the mouth.

A. Describe the process for the development of dental caries as it involves the interactions between host, diet, and bacterial flora:

pellicle formation—

plaque formation—

acid production—

localization—

enamel etching—

B. Mineralization of plaque produces calculus, which serves to mechanically irritate the gingiva and produce inflammation. Identify the microorganisms involved in causing further inflammation and tissue damage leading to periodontitis.

VII. SELF-TEST

1. *Treponema pallidum* is a strict parasite with such complex growth requirements that attempts to culture on artificial media have failed.
   a. True
   b. False

2. Syphilis is communicable during the
   a. primary stage.
   b. secondary stage.
   c. tertiary stage.
   d. primary and secondary stages.
   e. latency and tertiary stages.

3. Once the syphilis chancre heals spontaneously, the individual is disease free.
   a. True
   b. False

4. Lyme disease, producing the early symptom of a bull's-eye rash, is nonfatal, though it may evolve into cardiac dysrhythmias and neurological symptoms.
   a. True
   b. False

5. Most rickettsias are spread to humans by vectors. Which organism is the exception, and is spread primarily through nonvector means such as food, air, fomites, and animal products?
   a. *Rickettsia typhi*
   b. *R. rickettsii*
   c. *R. prowazekii*
   d. *Rochalimaea quintana*
   e. *Coxiella burnettii*

6. Since laboratory verification of rickettsial disease is time-consuming and immediate treatment is required, clinical observation and patient history are essential. Evidence sufficiently suggestive to start antimicrobial therapy includes
   a. the presence of a cluster of symptoms, including sudden fever, headache, and rash.
   b. recent contact with ticks or dogs.
   c. having possible occupational or recreational exposure in spring or summer.
   d. all of the above.
   e. none of the above.

7. *Chlamydia*, associated with venereal disease, always occur as the only infecting organism and therefore, are easily treated with penicillin.
   a. True
   b. False

8. The most prevalent of all sexually transmitted diseases is (are)
   a. gonorrhea.
   b. syphilis.
   c. chlamydial infections.
   d. venereal herpes.
   e. mycoplasmal infections.

9. Tetracycline and erythromycin inhibit mycoplasmal growth. With treatment, the symptoms rapidly diminish, but the infected person continues to shed viable organisms. To avoid relapse, treatment should be continued for
   a. 0 to 7 days.
   b. 7 to 14 days.
   c. 14 to 21 days.
   d. 21 to 28 days.
   e. none of the above.

10. Dental caries usually occur in
    _____ and periodontal infections
    in _____ .
    a. children, teenagers
    b. teenagers, children
    c. teenagers, adults
    d. adults, teenagers
    e. children, adults

11. The primary lesion at the site of inoculation
    in syphilis is the
    a. abscess.
    b. bubo.
    c. chancre.
    d. chancroid.
    e. rash.

12. The organism that causes syphilis,
    Treponema pallidum, is transmitted through
    a. casual contact.
    b. air droplets.
    c. fomites.
    d. unprotected sex with an infected
       individual.
    e. common vehicle.

13. The vector for Lyme disease is
    a. *Borrelia burgdorferi.*
    b. deer.
    c. *Ixodes* tick.
    d. white-footed mouse.
    e. man.

14. People who die from cholera suffer from
    a. starvation.
    b. meningitis.
    c. venereal disease.
    d. sepsis.
    e. dehydration.

15. _____ is the causative agent for
    Rocky Mountain spotted fever.
    a. *Rickettsia rickettsii*
    b. *R. typhi*
    c. *R. prowazekii*
    d. *Orientia tsutsugamushi*
    e. *Ehrlichia chaffeensis*

16. The vector of Rocky Mountain spotted
    fever is
    a. *Rickettsia rickettsii.*
    b. fleas.
    c. mites.
    d. lice.
    e. *Dermacentor andersoni.*

17. _____ causes primary atypical
    pneumonia.
    a. *Chlamydia trachomatis*
    b. *Mycoplasma pneumoniae*
    c. *Leptospira interrogans*
    d. *Vibrio parahaemolyticus*
    e. *Campylobacter jejuni*

18. Many times in a person diagnosed with a
    sexually transmitted disease, a second
    sexually transmitted disease will be present
    as well.
    a. True
    b. False

19. *Chlamydia* infection is the most prevalent
    of the sexually transmitted diseases,
    unfortunately there is no treatment and
    cure.
    a. True
    b. False

20. *Rickettsia* and *Chlamydia* grow well in
    artificial media because they are obligate
    intracellular parasites.
    a. True
    b. False

22 The Fungi of Medical Importance

OVERVIEW

Fungi are only somewhat medically important with their primary role in the earth's ecological balance including their impact on agriculture. Fungal disease (mycoses) may be separated into systemic, cutaneous, and subcutaneous categories. Respiratory allergies and diseases associated with toxin ingestion are also attributed to the fungi.

I. INTRODUCTION

Concept: Fungi are to some extent medically important as agents in human disease, allergies, and intoxications due to ingesting fungal toxins.

II. FUNGI AS INFECTIOUS AGENTS

Concept: Fungi are widely distributed; due to the relative resistance of humans and the fact that fungi are comparatively nonpathogenic, most exposures do not lead to infection (mycosis).

   Objective 1. Differentiate between true and opportunistic fungi.
   Objective 2. Characterize mycoses with respect to their epidemiology, pathogenesis, and diagnosis.

A. Contrast true and opportunistic fungal pathogens.

B. Identify the exceptions to the statement: Most fungal infections are not communicable.

   List some predisposing factors for fungal infections.

   Describe the significance of the interactions among the:

   fungal portal of entry—

   nature of the infectious dose—

   virulence of the fungus—

   host resistance—

Fungal identification can be accomplished by wet mounts and isolation on solid media. Media recommended for fungal isolation include Sabouraud's dextrose agar, mycosel agar, inhibitory mold medium, and brain-heart-infusion agar. State the purpose of the following media modifications:

addition of blood—

addition of chloramphenicol and gentamicins—

addition of cycloheximide—

III. SYSTEMIC INFECTIONS BY TRUE PATHOGENS

Concept: Airborne fungal spores enter the respiratory tract and produce a mild pulmonary infection that may become systemic, creating severe chronic lesions.

      Objective 1. Characterize the most common true pathogen, *Histoplasma capsulatum,* and its disease process.
      Objective 2. Characterize coccidioidomycosis.
      Objective 3. Characterize blastomycosis.

A.   Identify the distribution of the fungus *H. capsulatum.*

Describe the array of manifestation of histoplasmosis (include both benign and severe descriptions).

B.   The organism _____ _____, the etiologic agent of coccidioidomycosis, is probably the most virulent of all mycotic pathogens.

Describe these characteristics of *Coccidoides immitis:*

habitat—

dispersal—

persons at risk—

symptoms—

diagnosis—

prevention—

C. Describe the characteristics of *Blastomyces dermatitidis:*

habitat—

incidence—

transmission—

symptoms—

diagnosis—

treatment—

IV. SUBCUTANEOUS MYCOSES

Concept: Subcutaneous mycoses are progressive infections of the tissues within or just below the skin.

Objective 1. Discuss two fungal infections of the skin.

A. Who are more likely to contract sporotrichosis, and what precautions should be taken to avoid infection?

Barefooted men of rural occupation in the American subtropics are vulnerable to _____, a disease producing painless lesions that tend to be ignored.

_____ causes localized abscesses that, if untreated, lead to deformation of the affected body part, with pain and loss of function.

V. CUTANEOUS MYCOSES

Concept: Dermatophytoses are fungal infections of the nonliving epidermal tissues and their derivatives (hair and nails).

Objective 1. Characterize the dermatophytoses.

A. Fill in the chart.

Latin name	Area of body affected	Mode of acquisition	Pathologic appearance
Tinea capitis			
Tinea barbae			
Tinea corporis			
Tinea cruris			
Tinea pedis			
Tinea manuum			
Tinea unguium			

Explain the use of a Wood's light in diagnosing ringworm of the scalp.

State the methods suggested in treating ringworm and the basis for these methods.

VI. SUPERFICIAL MYCOSES

Concept: The innocuous superficial mycoses, occupying the outer epidermal surface, are generally of only cosmetic concern.

VII. OPPORTUNISTIC MYCOSES

Concept: Opportunistic fungi of humans include the yeasts *Candida, Cryptococcus,* and *Pneumocystis,* as well as the fungus *Aspergillus.*

Objective 1. Discuss the infections of *Candida.*
Objective 2. Characterize cryptococcosis.
Objective 3. Describe the persons susceptible to *Pneumocystis carinii* pneumonia and the symptoms of their disease.
Objective 4. Distinguish between noninvasive and invasive *Aspergillus* infections.

A. List the conditions that would encourage the invasion of an organism sometimes present in the normal flora, *Candida albicans.*

Contrast thrush and vulvovaginal candidiasis.

Discuss infections of other organs/structures by *Candida.*

Identify the recommended treatment for *Candida:*

superficial mucocutaneous infection—

systemic infection—

B. Though *Cryptococcus neoformans* is prevalent in urban areas where pigeons congregate, healthy humans have a strong resistance to it. The rate of cryptococcosis is highest among which persons?

The highest prevalence of cryptococcosis in the world is in the _____.

Contrast pulmonary and systemic cryptococcosis.

C. Identify the people who are most susceptible to *Pneumocystis carinii.*

List the symptoms of pneumocystis pneumonia.

D. Indicate the structures colonized with *Aspergillus* infections:

noninvasive—

invasive—

VIII. FUNGAL ALLERGIES AND INTOXICATIONS

Concept: Fungal hypersensitivities pose a potential health risk. Airborne spore counts are significant enough to be included in the televised weather broadcasts.

IX. SELF-TEST

1. Fungal pathogens that are not inherently invasive but can grow when inoculated into skin wounds or abrasions of healthy persons are considered
   a. true pathogens.
   b. opportunists.
   c. nonpathogenic.
   d. a cross between a and b.
   e. none of the above.

2. Few specific prevention measures exist for fungal infections.
   a. True
   b. False

3. The organism that causes histoplasmosis grows most abundantly in soil
   a. high in nitrogen.
   b. supplemented by bird droppings.
   c. supplemented by bat droppings.
   d. with adequate moisture.
   e. with all of the above.

4. Acute histoplasmosis generally leaves no residual effect, but a more serious, chronic form arises in
   a. teenagers.
   b. young adults.
   c. hosts lacking some important component of immune defense.
   d. persons living in the Ohio Valley.
   e. females.

5. The principal drug used in treating most of the mycoses is
   a. penicillin.
   b. erythromycin.
   c. tetracycline.
   d. amphotericin B.
   e. none of the above.

6. The dermatophytes that cause cutaneous mycoses are each very distinctive morphologically and easy to differentiate.
   a. True
   b. False

7. Ringworm of the scalp is transmitted from
   a. human to human.
   b. animal to human.
   c. soil to human.
   d. a and b.
   e. a and c.

8. The increased glucose content of the tissues and secretions of diabetics encourages the overgrowth of opportunistic fungi.
   a. True
   b. False

9. Significant fungal allergies include
   a. asthma.
   b. farmer's lung.
   c. teapicker's lung.
   d. bark stripper's disease.
   e. all of the above.

10. Which of the following is a true (primary) pathogen of humans?
    a. *Pneumocystis carinii*
    b. *Histoplasma capsulatum*
    c. *Candida albicans*
    d. *Aspergillus niger*
    e. all of the above

11. True pathogenic fungal infections usually involve the
    a. brain.
    b. skin.
    c. lung.
    d. liver.
    e. heart.

12. Most fungal infections are not communicable with the exceptions of some dermatophytes and *Candida*.
    a. True
    b. False

13. Most cases of fungal disease are diagnosed and reported to the CDC for monitoring.
    a. True
    b. False

14. The human body has antifungal defenses including
    a. normal integrity of the skin.
    b. mucous membranes.
    c. inflammatory response.
    d. phagocytosis.
    e. all of the above.

15. Accurate diagnosis of fungal disease requires all of the following except
    a. direct microscopic examination of fresh specimens.
    b. isolation on solid media.
    c. biochemical tests for the presence of enzymes.
    d. serological tests for host antibody.
    e. genetic analysis.

16. Immunization is not usually effective against fungal infections; prevention involves reducing contact with spores.
    a. True
    b. False

17. *Microsporum* grows well in/on all of these except the
    a. hair.
    b. genitals.
    c. skin.
    d. blood.
    e. feet.

18. In infants and the elderly, *Candida* causes
    a. pneumonia.
    b. vaginitis.
    c. thrush
    d. cystitis.
    e. septicemia.

19. A disease caused by a fungus is a mycosis.
    a. True
    b. False

20. A positive skin test for *Histoplasma capsulatum* concludes current infection.
    a. True
    b. False

23 The Parasites of Medical Importance

OVERVIEW

Protozoan infections are categorized by the type of motility (ameba, ciliate, flagellate) or lack of motility (apicomplexan) in the adult stage and the complexity of the infectious agent's life cycle. The helminths are macroscopic, multicellular worms that have microscopic infective forms (eggs and larvae). Helminths are categorized as roundworms and flatworms, with the flatworms further subdivided into the flukes and tapeworms.

I. INTRODUCTION

Concept: The eucaryotic parasites, the protozoa and helminths, are found everywhere due to rapid travel, immigration, and an increased number of immunocompromised persons.

II. TYPICAL PROTOZOAN PATHOGENS

Concept: The protozoans are divided into four groups (amebas, ciliates, flagellates, and sporozoans) based on mobility.

Objective 1. Characterize *E. histolytica* and its disease process.
Objective 2. Briefly discuss other amebas.
Objective 3. Discuss the pathogen *Balantidium coli* as it relates to human diseases.
Objective 4. Contrast the genera *Trichomonas, Giardia, Trypanosoma,* and *Leishmania* with respect to morphology, life cycle, pathogenesis, and control.
Objective 5. Identify the common characteristics of the sporozoans.
Objective 6. Characterize *Plasmodium* and the disease it causes: malaria.
Objective 7. Characterize the genera of the subclass Coccidia with emphasis on the genus *Toxoplasma.*

A. Enumerate the metamorphic forms of *E. histolytica* from the active, feeding stage to the dormant stage.

Describe the principal mode of infection of *E. histolytica.*

Recall the incidence of *E. histolytica* infections.

Name the primary target tissue of *E. histolytica.*

Diagnosis of *E. histolytica* requires microscopic examination of _____ specimens.

Along with symptomatic treatment of diarrhea and cramps, the drug of choice to treat *E. histolytica* infections is _____.

Discuss the prevention and control of *E. histolytica:*

in the community—

individually—

B.   Identify the portal of entry for *Naegleria fowleri.*

Review the incubation time, symptoms, and prognosis of *N. fowleri.*

Identify the portal of entry for *Acanthamoeba* sp.

Compare and contrast the disease produced and the speed of the disease process of *Naegleria* and *Acanthamoeba.*

C.   Describe these characteristics of *B. coli:*

size—

shape—

arrangement of cilia—

habitat—

transmission—

symptoms—

treatment—

D.   How many flagella are found associated with a trichomonad?

Explain the lack of vectors in the transmission of *Trichomonas* by close contact.

List symptoms of *Trichomonas vaginalis* in the:

male—

female—

Outline the life cycle of *Giardia lamblia* involving one host: the human.

Describe the structure of a trypomastigote, a form common to all trypanosomes sometime in their life cycle.

Which form of the *Leishmania* is flagellated?

Explain how *T. brucei* can be transmitted actively by a biologic vector or passively by a mechanical vector.

Identify the symptoms of both the early and late stages of African sleeping sickness *(Trypanosoma brucei)*.

Humans are not considered natural reservoirs of *Leishmania*. Name some of the principal reservoirs of this protozoan.

Contrast the three clinical forms of leishmaniasis with respect to symptoms and complications.

Control of mastigophoran disease is directed toward reducing the reservoir. Propose various methods aimed at achieving this goal.

E. List the common features of all sporozoans.

F. Describe the two phases in the life cycle of *Plasmodium.*

    asexual phase (human)—

    sexual phase (mosquito)—

    Identify the type of immunity developed from contracting malaria.

    Explain the significance of the genetic disorder sickle-cell anemia as it relates to malaria.

    Recount the symptoms of malaria, and describe how they are produced in the body.

    What drugs are used to treat malaria?

    Summarize the protective measures used to control the spread of malaria.

G. Contrast the life cycles of *Plasmodium* and the Coccidia.

    Describe these characteristics of *Toxoplasma:*

    reservoir—

    transmission—

    symptoms—

    persons at risk—

III. A SURVEY OF HELMINTH PARASITES

Concept: Helminths are multicellular animals with specialized tissues and organs similar to the hosts they parasitize and can be grouped into three categories: nematodes (roundworms), trematodes (flukes), and cestodes (tapeworms).

> **Objective 1.** Generally discuss the epidemiology, life cycle, transmission, pathology, diagnosis, and control of helminth diseases.
> **Objective 2.** Distinguish between the different intestinal nematodes and the tissue nematodes.
> **Objective 3.** Characterize the blood, liver, and lung flukes.
> **Objective 4.** Compare and contrast the various tapeworms.

A. Contrast the definitive, intermediate, and transport hosts of helminths.

Define infestation.

In what regions do most of the cases of helminth diseases occur?

Describe the damage caused by helminth infection.

Why is it difficult to develop vaccines against helminths?

How are helminth diseases diagnosed?

Discuss the problems involved with treating helminth diseases.

B. For each of the following roundworms describe how the worm is contracted, the manifestation of the disease, and the prevention of infection:

<u>Intestinal nematodes</u>

Ascaris lumbricoides—

Trichuris trichiura—

Enterobius vermicularis—

Necator americanus—

Strongyloides stercoralis—

Trichinella spiralis—

Tissue nematodes

Wuchereria bancrofti—

Onchocerca volvulus—

C. Draw the life cycle of the blood fluke.

For each of the following flukes describe how the fluke is contracted, the manifestation of the disease, and the prevention of infection:

Schistosoma sp.—

Opisthorchis sinensis—

Fasciola hepatica—

Paragonimus westermani—

D. Draw a tapeworm and label the parts.

Draw the life cycle of the beef tapeworm.

For each of the following tapeworms describe how the worm is contracted, the manifestation of the disease, and the prevention of infection:

Taenia saginata—

Taenia solium—

IV. SELF-TEST

1. In some asymptomatic individuals healing of bowel lesions caused by *E. histolytica* keeps up with erosion, while in severe cases lesions extend to and injure other tissues.
   a. True
   b. False

2. The geographic distribution of *Naegleria fowleri* appears to be pools of water worldwide, though the cysts are easily killed by chlorination or salination of the water.
   a. True
   b. False

3. This protozoan is responsible for a sexually transmitted disease.
   a. *Giardia lamblia*
   b. *Entamoeba polecki*
   c. *Trichomonas vaginalis*
   d. *Trypanosoma brucei*
   e. none of the above

4. *Giardia* is not highly invasive; the target tissue is the
   a. liver.
   b. skin.
   c. lungs.
   d. duodenum.
   e. large intestine.

5. Diagnosis of malaria is achieved through direct identification of plasmodia in a
   a. fecal smear.
   b. sputum smear.
   c. stained blood smear.
   d. conjunctival smear.
   e. none of the above.

6. Since infection with toxoplasmosis during pregnancy may cause embryonic or fetal damage (stillbirths, congenital defects—brain damage, blindness), pregnant women should avoid contact with
   a. mosquitos.
   b. cat feces.
   c. raw sewage.
   d. ticks.
   e. all of the above.

7. The host that harbors the adult, sexually mature helminth is the
   a. transport host.
   b. intermediate host.
   c. secondary host.
   d. definitive host.
   e. none of the above.

8. Which helminth is ingested from contaminated fingers, food, or drink, and is usually asymptomatic but may cause irritability, nervousness, nausea, abdominal discomfort, or diarrhea?
   a. *Ascaris lumbricoides*
   b. *Trichuris trichiura*
   c. *Enterobius vermicularis*
   d. *Necator americanus.*
   e. *Strongyloides stercoralis.*

9. An intermediate host of *Opisthorchis sinensis* is the
   a. snail.
   b. cow.
   c. dog.
   d. cat.
   e. pig.

10. A reproductive segment of the tapeworm is the
   a. scolex.
   b. neck.
   c. strobila.
   d. proglottid.
   e. larva.

11. Initial diagnosis of amebic dysentery is
   a. microscopic examination of a fecal smear.
   b. radiographs of the intestine.
   c. serological testing for antibodies against amebas.
   d. evaluation of the patient's clinical history and risk factors.
   e. all of the above.

12. Treating trichomoniasis involves
   a. oral treatment with metronidazole for three weeks.
   b. oral and vaginal treatment with metronidazole for one week.
   c. treatment of the sex partner (male or female) infected with *Trichomonas vaginalis* only.
   d. treatment of the entire family with metronidazole.
   e. none of the above.

13. *Giardia lamblia* is killed by all except
   a. boiling.
   b. ozone.
   c. iodine.
   d. chlorine.
   e. none of the above.

14. Trypanosomiasis involves pathogenic effects in the
   a. genitals.
   b. lungs.
   c. blood.
   d. liver.
   e. brain.

15. The causative agent of malaria is
   a. *Trichomonas vaginalis.*
   b. *Giardia lamblia.*
   c. *Plasmodium vivax.*
   d. *Trypanosoma brucei.*
   e. *Toxoplasma gondii.*

16. Snails are commonly the intermediate hosts of
   a. whipworms.
   b. pinworms.
   c. hookworms.
   d. flukes.
   e. tapeworms.

17. Which of these helminths only requires humans in its life cycle?
   a. pinworm
   b. blood fluke
   c. liver fluke
   d. lung fluke
   e. beef tapeworm

18. An increase in which type of white blood cell is common to helminth infestation?
   a. neutrophils
   b. eosinphils
   c. basophils
   d. monocytes
   e. lymphocytes

19. Definitive evidence of worm infestation is
    a. eosinophilia.
    b. serological tests.
    c. the discovery of eggs, larvae, or adult worms in stools, sputum, urine, gastric washings, blood, or tissue biopsies.
    d. history of travel to the tropics.
    e. immigration from infested areas.

20. Trematodes are tapeworms.
    a. True
    b. False

24 Introduction to the Viruses of Medical Importance: The DNA Viruses

OVERVIEW

Viruses depend on host cells for their qualities of life. Various viruses target nearly all types of tissues. The DNA viruses are assembled and budded off the nucleus of the target cell. Viral diseases can be very mild to severe. Antiviral chemotherapeutic agents are available. Prevention from several viral infections is vaccination.

I. INTRODUCTION

Concept: Viruses are obligate intracellular parasites and probably the most common infectious agents.

II. VIRUSES IN INFECTION AND DISEASE

Concept: The viruses—probably the most common infectious agents—are small packaged particles of DNA or RNA that are dependent on the host (animal, plant, or bacterial) cell for their qualities of life.

Objective 1.   Propose some general statements about viruses and their medical impact.

A.   Discuss the affinity of a virus for a specific target cell.

The scope of viral infections ranges from mild or asymptomatic to severe or deadly infections. Provide some examples of each of these extremes.

List some of the nonspecific, commonplace symptoms of viral infections.

How does the body protect itself from viral infections?

Define oncogenesis.

Relate teratogenicity to the occurrence of congenital defects.

Name two infections that may be transmitted to neonates at the time of birth.

List methods used to diagnose viral diseases.

III. ENVELOPED DNA VIRUSES

Concept: The enveloped DNA viruses include the poxviruses, the herpesviruses, and the hepadnaviruses.

Objective 1. Discuss the poxviruses using the representative disease smallpox.
Objective 2. Review the family of herpesviruses, including herpes simplex 1 and 2, herpes zoster, cytomegalovirus, and Epstein-Barr virus.
Objective 3. Characterize the hepadnaviruses.

A. Identify the poxvirus responsible for smallpox.

Describe the lesions produced by poxvirus.

Why was vaccination against smallpox discontinued?

B. Describe these characteristics common to the family of herpesviruses:

viral latency and recurrent infections—

structure—

site of replication—

viral release—

Contrast herpes simplex 1 and 2:

reservoir—

transmission—

triggers for recurrent infection—

target tissues—

diagnosis by tissue culture—

treatment—

prevention—

Identify the location of infection:

herpes gingivostomatitis—

herpes labialis—

herpes keratitis—

Enumerate the symptoms of herpes simplex 2.

Detail two ways herpes simplex 2 is transmitted to the newborn.

Explain the acquisition of whitlow (an abscess on the distal portion of a phalanx).

Name the two diseases caused by the same herpesvirus, varicella-zoster virus.

Describe communication of the varicella-zoster virus.

Outline the pattern of infection and disease for:

chickenpox—

shingles—

Identify factors responsible for the reactivation of the varicella-zoster virus.

Explain how cytomegaloviruses received their name.

List the modes of transmission of cytomegalovirus.

Though most healthy adults and children with primary cytomegalovirus infection are asymptomatic, describe the disease as it affects the fetus, newborn, and immunodeficient adult who develop a more virulent form.

Name the two diseases caused by the Epstein-Barr virus.

Identify the site of Epstein-Barr virus replication.

Fill in the chart.

	Manifestation	Treatment
infectious mononucleosis		
Burkitt's lymphoma		

C.   Contrast the resistance and sensitivity of the hepatitis B virus.

Describe these characteristics of the hepatits B virus:

transmission—

incidence/persons at risk—

target tissue—

symptoms—

treatment—

prevention—

IV. NONENVELOPED DNA VIRUSES

Concept: Nonenveloped DNA viruses include the adenoviruses and the papovaviruses.

Objective 1. Indicate the persons at risk of contracting an adenovirus and the symptoms of the diseases produced by infection.
Objective 2. Discuss papilloma viruses as they relate to human warts.

A.   Who is at a greater risk of contracting adenovirus?

Symptoms associated with respiratory, gastrointestinal, and ocular infection with adenovirus include:

B.   Matching.

___ prevalent STD linked to some types of cancer a.   common (seed) warts
___ painless, elevated, rough growths on the fingers b.   plantar warts
___ deep, painful papillomas on the soles of the feet c.   genital warts

Describe the various methods of wart transmission.

V. PARVOVIRUSES: NONENVELOPED, SINGLE-STRANDED DNA VIRUSES

Concept: Parvoviruses are indigenous to and may cause disease in cats (distemper), dogs (enteric disease), and humans (B19).

VI. SELF-TEST

1. Viruses are divided into families based on
    a. the nature of the nucleic acid within the viral particle.
    b. the type of capsid.
    c. the presence or absence of an envelope.
    d. all of the above.
    e. none of the above.

2. The immunity that results from a viral infection is
    a. short-term.
    b. life-long.
    c. passive.
    d. innate.
    e. none of the above.

3. Worldwide eradication of which disease has been accomplished by the World Health Organization (WHO)?
    a. smallpox
    b. herpes simplex 1 (fever blisters)
    c. herpes simplex 2 (genital infections)
    d. hepatitis B
    e. chickenpox

4. Circulating antibodies to herpes simplex produced during the primary infection appear to account for the relative mildness of subsequent attacks, but are not fully successful in preventing latency or reinfection.
    a. True
    b. False

5. Patients with shingles are a source of infection for children even though the children have experienced previous infection with the varicella-zoster virus.
    a. True
    b. False

6. The natural habitat of the Epstein-Barr virus is the human
    a. epithelium.
    b. nasopharynx.
    c. lymphoid tissue and salivary glands.
    d. stomach and intestinal mucosa.
    e. none of the above.

7. What causes jaundice in the hepatitis patient?
    a. necrosis of hepatocytes
    b. interference with the excretion of bile pigments into the intestine
    c. bilirubin accumulating in the blood and tissues
    d. inflammation of the liver, disruption of liver structure
    e. all of the above

8. A vaccine is available to protect persons at risk of contracting
    a. herpes simplex 1.
    b. herpes simplex 2.
    c. shingles.
    d. papilloma virus.
    e. hepatitis B (HBV).

9. Adenoviruses were first isolated from the
    a. liver.
    b. salivary glands.
    c. appendix.
    d. adrenals.
    e. adenoids.

10. Which of these viruses is a known oncogen?
    a. varicella-zoster virus
    b. hepadnavirus
    c. adenovirus
    d. papilloma virus
    e. none of the above

11. The significant source of herpes simplex infection is
    a. inhalation of virus in contaminated air.
    b. ingestion of virus in contaminated food.
    c. contaminated fomites.
    d. direct contact with active lesions.
    e. all of the above.

12. Which of the following is an example of teratogenic infection?
    a. chicken pox
    b. rubella
    c. herpes simplex 1
    d. herpes simplex 2
    e. hepatitis B

13. Fever blisters recur because
    a. the person who was previously infected becomes reinfected.
    b. several different viruses can cause fever blisters.
    c. the latent virus that caused the original infection is reactivated.
    d. circulating viral particles occasionally find suitable receptors.
    e. all of the above.

14. Herpes simplex 2 infection includes all of the following symptoms except
    a. urethritis.
    b. painful urination.
    c. itching.
    d. central nervous system involvement.
    e. fever blisters.

15. Viruses cause less disease than bacteria or fungi.
    a. True
    b. False

16. Reactivation of latent herpes virus infection is triggered by
    a. fever.
    b. ultraviolet radiation.
    c. stress.
    d. mechanical injury.
    e. all of the above.

17. The most effective treatment for herpes virus is
    a. acyclovir.
    b. penicillin.
    c. metronidazole.
    d. vidarabine.
    e. ampicillin.

18. There are no more smallpox viruses in the world.
    a. True
    b. False

19. Mothers who are carriers of hepatitis B virus are highly likely to transmit infection to their newborns during delivery.
    a. True
    b. False

20. Shingles (Herpes zoster) produces symptoms including
    a. skin rash.
    b. skin vesicles.
    c. skin vesicles and inflammation of the ganglia.
    d. fever blisters.
    e. jaundice.

25   RNA Viruses of Medical Importance

OVERVIEW

The RNA viruses have the potential of becoming the most important disease threats of the future. RNA viruses include the viral agents of influenza, mumps, measles, rabies, rubella, AIDS, polio, and the common cold. Though differing in structure with respect to their envelope, capsid, and RNA genome, all RNA viruses multiply in and are released from the cytoplasm of their target cells.

I.   INTRODUCTION

Concept: RNA viruses are the agents in a number of serious and prevalent human diseases.

II.   ENVELOPED, SEGMENTED, SINGLE-STRANDED RNA VIRUSES

Concept: The enveloped, single-stranded RNA viruses include the orthomyxoviruses, the bunyaviruses, and the arenaviruses.

Objective 1.   Characterize the orthomyxovirus influenza.
Objective 2.   Discuss the zoonotic diseases produced by the bunyaviruses and arenaviruses.

A.   Name and describe the function of the two glycoproteins that comprise the spikes of the influenza viral lipoprotein envelope.

Define antigenic drift.

Define antigenic shift.

Describe these characteristics of influenza:

transmission—

occurrence—

symptoms—

complications—

treatment—

prevention—

B. Though not natural parasites of humans, the bunyaviruses and arenaviruses may be transmitted zoonotically. Indicate the vector(s) and the disease(s) of:

bunyaviruses—

arenaviruses—

III. ENVELOPED, NONSEGMENTED, SINGLE-STRANDED RNA VIRUSES

Concept: The paramyxoviruses possess HN and F spikes that are responsible for producing the cytoplasmic effect of a multinucleate giant cell. Few of the rhabdoviruses affect humans.

Objective 1. Distinguish parainfluenza, a more benign disease process, from influenza.
Objective 2. Characterize the mumps disease process.
Objective 3. Characterize measles (rubeola) caused by *Morbillivirus*—not to be confused with rubella caused by a togavirus.
Objective 4. Discuss respiratory syncytial virus (RSV) as it relates to the highly susceptible children of less than one year of age.
Objective 5. Characterize rabies, one of the few rhabdoviruses that affects humans.

A. Contrast cold and croup, symptoms of parainfluenza.

B. Describe these characteristics of mumps:

natural hosts—

transmission—

symptoms—

complications—

treatment—

prevention—

C. Describe these characteristics of measles (rubeola):

reservoir—

transmission—

conditions that favor epidemic spread—

symptoms—

complications—

treatment—

prevention—

D. Contrast the symptoms of RSV in the infant with those in the older child and adult.

E. Reservoirs of rabies include:

Describe the course of rabies, from exposure to CNS involvement.

Contrast the furious and the dumb forms of rabies.

Relate the laboratory criteria for diagnosing rabies.

Outline the steps of postexposure prophylaxis.

Explain the prescribed measures of rabies prevention and control.

IV. OTHER ENVELOPED RNA VIRUSES

Concept: The coronaviruses are common in domesticated animals, as well as being implicated in some human respiratory and intestinal infections. The togaviruses include the rubiviruses (agents of rubella) and the arboviruses (spread by arthropod vectors).

> **Objective 1.** Characterize rubella.
> **Objective 2.** Characterize the arthropod-borne viruses (arboviruses), including the fevers and encephalitides they cause.

A. Identify the two clinical forms of rubella.

Though half of all postnatal rubella infections are asymptomatic, describe the development of symptoms if they occur.

What is the severity of damage of congenital rubella dependent upon?

List the varieties of damage caused by congenital rubella infection in the first trimester of pregnancy.

B. Describe these characteristics of arthropod vectors and arboviruses:

major vectors—

factors affecting longevity of the arthropod—

peak incidence of disease—

symptoms of febrile illness—

symptoms of encephalitis—

treatment—

prevention—

control of infection—

List the names of the arboviral diseases:

encephalitides—

fevers—

V. ENVELOPED SINGLE-STRANDED RNA VIRUSES WITH REVERSE TRANSCRIPTASE: RETROVIRUSES

Concept: Retroviruses, like the human immunodeficiency virus (HIV), have known oncogenic abilities, often cause fatal diseases (AIDS), and are capable of reprogramming a host's DNA (converting a single-stranded RNA into a double-stranded viral DNA).

Objective 1. Characterize AIDS.
Objective 2. Discuss the significance of other retroviral diseases in humans.

A. Outline a brief history of AIDS.

Describe these characteristics of AIDS:

transmission—

symptoms—

target cells—

diagnosis—

treatment—

prevention—

What does it mean if a person is seropositive for AIDS?

List the groups more likely to contract AIDS (in order of prevalence).

Describe the progression of HIV infection.

Discuss the primary effect of AIDS.

Relate the secondary effects of AIDS, including opportunistic infections and associated cancers.

B.   Adult T-cell leukemia is caused by another retrovirus. Name the virus.

Retrovirus HTLV I has been isolated from persons with other diseases. These include:

VI. NONENVELOPED, NONSEGMENTED, SINGLE-STRANDED RNA VIRUSES: PICORNAVIRUSES AND CALICIVIRUSES

Concept: Representatives of this group of viruses are the enteroviruses (including the poliovirus and hepatitis A virus), the rhinoviruses, and the caliciviruses.

Objective 1.   Characterize poliomyelitis.
Objective 2.   Characterize nonpolio enteroviruses, including hepatitis A.
Objective 3.   Characterize the rhinoviruses.

A.   Explain the basis for the stability and resistance of the poliovirus.

Discuss the transmission of polio.

List and describe the four courses of polio infection.

Describe the two forms of polio vaccine currently in use.

B.   Though recovery is usually complete, describe some of the important complications of nonpolio enteroviruses.

Describe these characteristics of the hepatitis A virus:

transmission—

causes in U.S.—

reservoirs—

symptoms—

target cells—

Relate the use of immune serum globulin in the treatment and prophylaxis of the hepatitis A virus.

C.   Rhinoviruses are associated with the _____ _____.

Explain the significance of protuberance and indentation antigens with respect to why immunity to rhinovirus is so elusive.

Describe these characteristics of rhinovirus:

transmission—

incubation time—

symptoms—

treatment—

prevention—

VII. NONENVELOPED, SEGMENTED, DOUBLE-STRANDED RNA VIRUSES: REOVIRUSES

Concept: *Reovirus* is not considered a significant human pathogen, while *Rotavirus* is a significant cause of human infantile diarrhea.

VIII. SLOW INFECTIONS BY UNCONVENTIONAL VIRUSLIKE AGENTS

Concept: Transmissible, uniformly fatal, chronic infections of the nervous system of this group include kuru and Creutzfeldt-Jakob disease.

IX. SELF-TEST

1. Influenza is seasonal, occurring in the
   a. late winter and spring.
   b. late spring and summer.
   c. late summer and fall.
   d. late fall and winter.
   e. none of the above.

2. Long-lasting immunity follows any form of mumps infection, even the commonly occurring subclinical cases.
   a. True
   b. False

3. Koplik's spots are
   a. red maculopapular exantham.
   b. unusual oral lesions, characteristic of mumps.
   c. unusual oral lesions, characteristic of measles (rubella).
   d. unusual oral lesions, characteristic of measles (rubeola).
   e. none of the above.

4. In order to transmit the rubella virus to her fetus, the mother must be expressing symptoms of the infection.
   a. True
   b. False

5. Symptoms of encephalitis are extremely variable, including
   a. convulsions.
   b. paralysis.
   c. tremor.
   d. palsies.
   e. all of the above.

6. Many persons with AIDS have not yet begun to show symptoms because they are in the _____ phase of the disease.
   a. decline
   b. prodromal
   c. latent
   d. illness
   e. convalescent

7. A nursing baby can receive the AIDS virus from its mother or give the AIDS virus to its mother.
   a. True
   b. False

8. Opportunistic infections in the AIDS patient involve
   a. *Pneumocystis carinii.*
   b. fungi *(Candida albicans).*
   c. viruses (herpesvirus).
   d. bacteria *(Mycobacterium).*
   e. all of the above.

9. To diagnose polio, it must be distinguished from similar diseases including all *except*
   a. Guillain-Barre syndrome.
   b. infant botulism.
   c. tetanus.
   d. encephalitis.
   e. none of the above.

10. This virus is believed to cause one-third of all cases of viral gastroenteritis (nausea, vomiting, cramps, diarrhea, and chills).
    a. polio virus
    b. Norwalk virus
    c. hepatitis A virus
    d. *Coxsackievirus*
    e. *Echovirus*

11. Infection with rabies is usually the result of
    a. inhalation of viral particles.
    b. ingestion of viral particles.
    c. bite of an infected animal.
    d. touching of an infected animal.
    e. all of the above.

12. Influenza infection in the elderly is many times complicated by
    a. encephalitis.
    b. viral pneumonia.
    c. bacterial pneumonia.
    d. central nervous system disorders.
    e. kidney disease.

13. Polio virus is transmitted by
    a. inhalation of viral particles.
    b. ingestion of viral particles.
    c. bite of an infected individual.
    d. sexual contact with infected
        individual.
    e. none of the above.

14. Vaccination is recommended for measles,
    mumps, and rubella (MMR).
    a. True
    b. False

15. The leading cause of morbidity and
    mortality in AIDS patients is
    a. *Candida albicans.*
    b. *Cryptococcus neoformans.*
    c. *Toxoplasma gondii.*
    d. *Pneumoncystis carinii.*
    e. *Cryptosporidium.*

16. Most common colds are caused by
    a. caliciviruses.
    b. rhinoviruses.
    c. reoviruses.
    d. rotaviruses.
    e. none of the above.

17. Amantadine is an antiviral drug used to
    treat influenza.
    a. True
    b. False

18. The most prevalent cause of respiratory
    infection in newborns is
    a. influenza virus.
    b. respiratory syncytial virus.
    c. rhinovirus.
    d. reovirus.
    e. rotavirus.

19. Rubella infection in the first trimester may
    cause
    a. cardiac abnormalities.
    b. ocular lesions.
    c. deafness.
    d. mental and physical retardation.
    e. all of the above.

20. Donating blood can expose the donor to
    AIDS.
    a. True
    b. False

26 Environmental and Applied Microbiology

OVERVIEW

Much emphasis is placed on the microbiology of disease while ignoring the roles of microbes in the soil and water as they interact with each other and the environment. This knowledge of roles microbes play in the environment and the application of microbes as used in the food, drug, and agricultural industries increase the quality of human life.

I. INTRODUCTION

Concept: Microbes are beneficial. They help maintain and control the life support systems on the earth.

II. ECOLOGY: THE INTERCONNECTING WEB OF LIFE

Concept: Environmental or ecological microbiology is the study of microbes in natural habitats, the many interactions between microbes and their environment taking place at many levels at any given moment.

Objective 1. Characterize an ecosystem with respect to organization, energy, and nutritional flow.
Objective 2. Discuss the microbial activities in the natural recycling of bioelements—carbon and nitrogen.
Objective 3. Review soil microbiology.
Objective 4. Summarize the characteristics of water, including the roles of microbes as part of the problem and solution of a safe water supply.

A. The all-encompassing biosphere (global ecosystem) is subdivided into two parts—terrestrial and aquatic. Indicate the further subdivisions of each of these two.

Fill in the puzzle on the following page.

Explain the significance of a food or energy pyramid as it corresponds to an ecosystem.

Contrast:

mutually beneficial vs. commensalism—

cometabolism vs. synergism—

parasitism vs. competition—

Across

5. A mixed assemblage of organisms that live together at the same place and time.
7. A feeding pathway.
10. A few miles into the air of the ecosystem.
11. The overall role a species (or population) serves in a community.
12. These provide the fundamental energy source for all levels of the trophic pyramids by producing organic carbon compounds from the inorganic carbon dioxide in the atmosphere.

Down

1. These eat the bodies of other living organisms and obtain energy from bonds present in organic substrates they contain.
2. The physical location in the environment to which an organism has adapted.
3. A few miles into the soil of the ecosystem.
4. A group of organisms of the same species.
6. The water found within the global ecosystem.
8. Break down and absorb the organic matter of dead organisms.
9. A multichannel food chain.

B. List the processes of carbon cycling through ecosystems.

A balance of carbon dioxide in the atmosphere is necessary for the efficient recycling of carbon. What is disturbing this balance?

What will be the impact of this imbalance?

In the carbon cycle, carbon dioxide is changed into a high-energy organic compound by the process of photosynthesis. Outline the major steps in the:

light reactions—

dark reactions—

Name the organisms responsible for the dominant oxygenic photosynthesis performed on earth.

Identify and describe the role of microbes in the four basic types of reactions in the nitrogen cycle.

C. Characterize a lichen and the role it plays in soil microbiology.

Characterize humus and the role it plays in soil microbiology.

What accounts for the variation in humus content?

How do humans increase the amount of humus in soil?

Describe the various relationships between soil microbes and plants.

Discuss the role of the soil decomposers.

D.   The water in the atmosphere comes from:

Water is returned to the earth through _____ or
_____.

Discuss how the distribution and quality of water has changed over the years.

Label the drawing showing zonation of a freshwater lake.

??? zone (open, deeper)   **??? zone (shoreline)**

land   **land**

??? zone

??? zone

??? zone

Oceans are similar to freshwater lakes except in their possession of tidal and wave factors, as well as an abyssal zone. What are the effects of these differences?

Contrast the presence of nutrients in the aquatic ecosystems:

oligotrophic—

eutrophic—

Discuss the mechanisms and complications of eutrophication.

Identify the pathogens featured most prominently in contaminated water.

Most of these pathogens are carried in feces. Evidence of fecal contamination has become the standard for microbiological analysis of water purity. Name the indicator bacteria routinely monitored.

Describe two methods for testing total bacteria levels:

standard plate count—

biochemical oxygen demand—

Outline the procedures for coliform enumeration.

Most probable number (MPN):

    presumptive—

    confirmatory—

    completed—

Membrane filter method—

Relate the stepwise process of water purification.

Provide the details, including microbial activity, of the three phases of sewage treatment:

primary stage—

secondary stage—

tertiary stage—

III. APPLIED MICROBIOLOGY AND BIOTECHNOLOGY

Concept: Applied microbiology is the study of practical uses of microbes in food processing, industrial production, and bioengineering.

Objective 1. Summarize the relationships between microorganisms and foods as detrimental, beneficial, or neutral to humans.
Objective 2. Characterize methods for preventing microbial food poisoning and spoilage.
Objective 3. Discuss the use of microorganisms in food production.
Objective 4. Illustrate the importance of the use of microorganisms for food.
Objective 5. Relate industrial microbiology to the bulk production of organic compounds.

A. Describe the effects of microbes on foods:

detrimental—

neutral—

beneficial—

Contrast food intoxication and food infection.

Indicate the most common food-borne illness in the U.S.

B. Discuss these measures aimed at preventing microbial food poisoning and spoilage:

preventing incorporation of microbes into foods—

preventing survival or multiplication of microbes into foods—

Review the use of temperature in food preservation, including heat for canning, cooking, and pasteurization, as well as the cold in refrigeration.

Relate the use of radiation, both gamma and cathode rays, in the sterilization and disinfection of foods.

Indicate several other forms of preservation and explain the basis for each form.

C. Describe the fermentation process from start to finish, including the organism(s) involved in each step of the process:

bread making—

alcoholic beverages

beer brewing—

wine making—

distilled beverages—

plant products

sauerkraut—

pickles—

vinegar—

milk and dairy products

      unripened cheese—

      ripened cheese—

      yogurt—

Contrast natural and controlled fermentation.

D.   Describe the historical use and plans for the future use of microorganisms for food.

E.   List the requirements to create a specific product with the aid of a microorganism.

Describe and provide examples of the two basic kinds of microbial metabolic products harvested by industrial processes:

primary metabolites—

secondary metabolites—

Contrast batch and continuous feed systems with respect to substance production by a fermentor.

Indicate the various products resulting from microbial biosynthesis.

IV. SELF-TEST

1. Biotic factors include any nonliving parts and surroundings of an ecosystem.
   a. True
   b. False

2. A predator is a form of
   a. producer that actively seeks out and ingests live prey.
   b. decomposer that actively seeks out and ingests live prey.
   c. consumer that actively seeks out and ingests live prey.
   d. commensal that actively seeks out and ingests live prey.
   e. none of the above.

3. In photosynthetic organisms, the function of the chlorophylls, carotenoids, and phycobilins is
   a. the absorbance of light (solar energy).
   b. the reflection of light.
   c. the production of energy (ATP).
   d. the absorbance of ATP.
   e. none of the above.

4. The porous structure of soil creates pockets for which both water and oxygen compete, thus
   a. saturated soils contain more oxygen.
   b. saturated soils contain less oxygen.
   c. dry soils contain less oxygen.
   d. dry soils contain more aerobes and facultative forms.
   e. none of the above.

5. Turnover occurs in larger bodies of standing water when water from the warm, upper regions mixes with water from the cooler, deeper regions, breaking down the thermocline.
   a. True
   b. False

6. The mass, controlled culture of microbes to produce desired organic compounds is called
   a. decomposition.
   b. synthesis.
   c. respiration.
   d. fermentation.
   e. metabolism.

7. All of the following are reasons for using the membrane filter method for water testing instead of the most probable number procedure to detect coliforms *except* it
   a. is faster.
   b. requires fewer steps.
   c. is more expensive.
   d. is more portable.
   e. can process larger quantities of water.

8. To inhibit the multiplication of bacteria in food served buffet style for an extended period, the holding temperature should be
   a. below 15°C or above 45°C.
   b. between 15°C and 45°C.
   c. between 4°C and 60°C.
   d. below 4°C or above 60°C.
   e. none of the above.

9. Coagulation of milk proteins to form curd is accomplished by
   a. lactose fermentation.
   b. microbial action.
   c. an enzyme from the stomach of unweaned calves.
   d. renin.
   e. all of the above.

10. Tricks of the trade employed by industrial microbiologists to increase the production of the chosen end product include
    a. the manipulation of the growth environment.
    b. the selection of microbial strains that genetically lack feedback systems to allow end products to accumulate.
    c. scaling up with a fermentor device.
    d. all of the above.
    e. none of the above.

Matching.

_____ 11. biosphere
_____ 12. lithosphere
_____ 13. communities
_____ 14. populations
_____ 15. habitat
_____ 16. niche

a. groups of organisms of the same species
b. overall role that a species serves
c. a few miles into the soil
d. physical location of the adapted organism in the environment
e. thin envelope of life (about 14 miles deep)
f. mixed assemblages of organism interrelating

17. The most important of the photosynthetic pigments are the
    a. chlorophylls.
    b. carotenoids.
    c. phycobilins.
    d. reds.
    e. all of the above.

18. Root nodules (special nitrogen-fixing organs) are formed when *rhizobia* infect legumes including all except
    a. soybeans.
    b. peas.
    c. squash.
    d. alfalfa.
    e. clover.

19. The unique zone where the river meets the sea that is high in nutrients, fluctuates in salinity, and supports a specialized microbial community is
    a. the photic zone.
    b. the profundal zone.
    c. the benthic zone.
    d. an estuary.
    e. the abyssal zone.

20. Reclaimed sewage water is usually used to water golf courses and parks, rather than for drinking.
    a. True
    b. False

Answers to the Self-Tests

Chapter 1
1.	b.	11.	e.
2.	c.	12.	b.
3.	b.	13.	a.
4.	d.	14.	b.
5.	e.	15.	d.
6.	d.	16.	e.
7.	a.	17.	a.
8.	d.	18.	b.
9.	b.	19.	d.
10.	e.	20.	c.

Chapter 2
1.	b.	11.	d.
2.	c.	12.	b.
3.	a.	13.	c.
4.	b.	14.	c.
5.	d.	15.	d.
6.	e.	16.	b.
7.	d.	17.	b.
8.	c.	18.	b.
9.	e.	19.	a.
10.	a.	20.	c.

Chapter 3
1.	c.	11.	d.
2.	b.	12.	d.
3.	b.	13.	a.
4.	e.	14.	a.
5.	c.	15.	e.
6.	d.	16.	b.
7.	b.	17.	d.
8.	b.	18.	b.
9.	a.	19.	c.
10.	e.	20.	e.

Chapter 4
1.	d.	11.	e.
2.	c.	12.	c.
3.	b.	13.	d.
4.	c.	14.	b.
5.	e.	15.	d.
6.	a.	16.	a.
7.	d.	17.	b.
8.	b.	18.	c.
9.	a.	19.	d.
10.	e.	20.	d.

Chapter 5
1.	c.	11.	d.
2.	b.	12.	b.
3.	a.	13.	b.
4.	e.	14.	b.
5.	c.	15.	b.
6.	b.	16.	d.
7.	a.	17.	a.
8.	d.	18.	c.
9.	d.	19.	b.
10.	a.	20.	d.

Chapter 6
1.	c.	11.	b.
2.	a.	12.	d.
3.	d.	13.	c.
4.	b.	14.	d.
5.	b.	15.	c.
6.	e.	16.	b.
7.	a.	17.	a.
8.	d.	18.	a.
9.	c.	19.	b.
10.	e.	20.	b.

Chapter 7
1.	a.	11.	c.
2.	d.	12.	a.
3.	c.	13.	b.
4.	d.	14.	d.
5.	a.	15.	d.
6.	b.	16.	b.
7.	c.	17.	d.
8.	c.	18.	a.
9.	b.	19.	e.
10.	e.	20.	c.

Chapter 8
1.	d.	11.	b.
2.	b.	12.	b.
3.	a.	13.	c.
4.	c.	14.	e.
5.	a.	15.	c.
6.	d.	16.	b.
7.	c.	17.	a.
8.	b.	18.	a.
9.	e.	19.	b.
10.	d.	20.	d.

Chapter 9
1.	b.	11.	e.
2.	c.	12.	e.
3.	a.	13.	d.
4.	d.	14.	e.
5.	b.	15.	c.
6.	e.	16.	b.
7.	d.	17.	b.
8.	b.	18.	d.
9.	a.	19.	b.
10.	e.	20.	e.

Chapter 10

1.	c.	11.	b.
2.	a.	12.	e.
3.	b.	13.	a.
4.	e.	14.	b.
5.	a.	15.	d.
6.	c.	16.	c.
7.	d.	17.	a.
8.	b.	18.	e.
9.	b.	19.	a.
10.	a.	20.	a.

Chapter 11

1.	d.	11.	b.
2.	b.	12.	c.
3.	a.	13.	e.
4.	c.	14.	e.
5.	c.	15.	b.
6.	b.	16.	e.
7.	a.	17.	c.
8.	e.	18.	a.
9.	d.	19.	b.
10.	b.	20.	d.

Chapter 12

1.	b.	11.	c.
2.	a.	12.	b.
3.	c.	13.	d.
4.	a.	14.	d.
5.	b.	15.	b.
6.	d.	16.	a.
7.	c.	17.	a.
8.	e.	18.	b.
9.	d.	19.	b.
10.	a.	20.	b.

Chapter 13

1.	b.	11.	d.
2.	d.	12.	e.
3.	c.	13.	b.
4.	a.	14.	a.
5.	e.	15.	c.
6.	b.	16.	c.
7.	d.	17.	a.
8.	e.	18.	d.
9.	b.	19.	d.
10.	c.	20.	b.

Chapter 14

1.	e.	11.	b.
2.	e.	12.	a.
3.	a.	13.	e.
4.	b.	14.	b.
5.	c.	15.	e.
6.	a.	16.	a.
7.	d.	17.	c.
8.	c.	18.	b.
9.	b.	19.	e.
10.	d.	20.	e.

Chapter 15

1.	b.	11.	d.
2.	a.	12.	b.
3.	c.	13.	d.
4.	d.	14.	e.
5.	b.	15.	a.
6.	a.	16.	c.
7.	c.	17.	d.
8.	e.	18.	d.
9.	d.	19.	b.
10.	c.	20.	b.

Chapter 16

1.	c.	11.	e.
2.	e.	12.	c.
3.	d.	13.	d.
4.	e.	14.	a.
5.	a.	15.	e.
6.	b.	16.	a.
7.	c.	17.	b.
8.	b.	18.	c.
9.	d.	19.	b.
10.	e.	20.	a.

Chapter 17

1.	b.	11.	a.
2.	a.	12.	e.
3.	c.	13.	b.
4.	b.	14.	b.
5.	e.	15.	d.
6.	d.	16.	a.
7.	c.	17.	e.
8.	a.	18.	c.
9.	d.	19.	a.
10.	e.	20.	c.

Introduction to Identification Techniques

1.	b.
2.	a.
3.	d.
4.	b.
5.	a.
6.	c.
7.	e.
8.	d.
9.	e.
10.	e.

Chapter 18

1.	d.	11.	b.
2.	c.	12.	a.
3.	d.	13.	b.
4.	c.	14.	e.
5.	e.	15.	b.
6.	b.	16.	e.
7.	a.	17.	a.
8.	e.	18.	b.
9.	b.	19.	a.
10.	b.	20.	d.

Chapter 19

1.	d.	11.	b.
2.	e.	12.	a.
3.	a.	13.	d.
4.	a.	14.	e.
5.	a.	15.	b.
6.	c.	16.	a.
7.	d.	17.	b.
8.	b.	18.	b.
9.	b.	19.	e.
10.	a.	20.	a.

Chapter 20

1.	c.	11.	d.
2.	a.	12.	c.
3.	b.	13.	d.
4.	a.	14.	b.
5.	b.	15.	d.
6.	d.	16.	e.
7.	d.	17.	c.
8.	c.	18.	e.
9.	e.	19.	c.
10.	c.	20.	a.

Chapter 21

1.	a.	11.	c.
2.	d.	12.	d.
3.	b.	13.	c.
4.	a.	14.	e.
5.	e.	15.	a.
6.	d.	16.	e.
7.	b.	17.	b.
8.	c.	18.	a.
9.	c.	19.	b.
10.	e.	20.	b.

Chapter 22

1.	c.	11.	c.
2.	a.	12.	a.
3.	e.	13.	b.
4.	c.	14.	e.
5.	d.	15.	c.
6.	b.	16.	a.
7.	d.	17.	d.
8.	a.	18.	c.
9.	e.	19.	a.
10.	b.	20.	b.

Chapter 23

1.	a.	11.	a.
2.	b.	12.	b.
3.	c.	13.	d.
4.	d.	14.	e.
5.	c.	15.	c.
6.	b.	16.	d.
7.	d.	17.	a.
8.	c.	18.	b.
9.	a.	19.	c.
10.	d.	20.	b.

Chapter 24

1.	d.	11.	d.
2.	b.	12.	b.
3.	a.	13.	c.
4.	a.	14.	e.
5.	b.	15.	b.
6.	c.	16.	e.
7.	c.	17.	a.
8.	e.	18.	b.
9.	e.	19.	a.
10.	d.	20.	c.

Chapter 25

1.	d.	11.	c.
2.	a.	12.	c.
3.	d.	13.	b.
4.	b.	14.	a.
5.	e.	15.	d.
6.	c.	16.	b.
7.	a.	17.	a.
8.	e.	18.	b.
9.	c.	19.	e.
10.	b.	20.	b.

Chapter 26

1.	b.	11.	e.
2.	c.	12.	c.
3.	a.	13.	f.
4.	b.	14.	a.
5.	a.	15.	d.
6.	d.	16.	b.
7.	c.	17.	a.
8.	d.	18.	c.
9.	e.	19.	d.
10.	d.	20.	a.